IMAGES
of America

WHITEMARSH HALL
THE ESTATE OF
EDWARD T. STOTESBURY

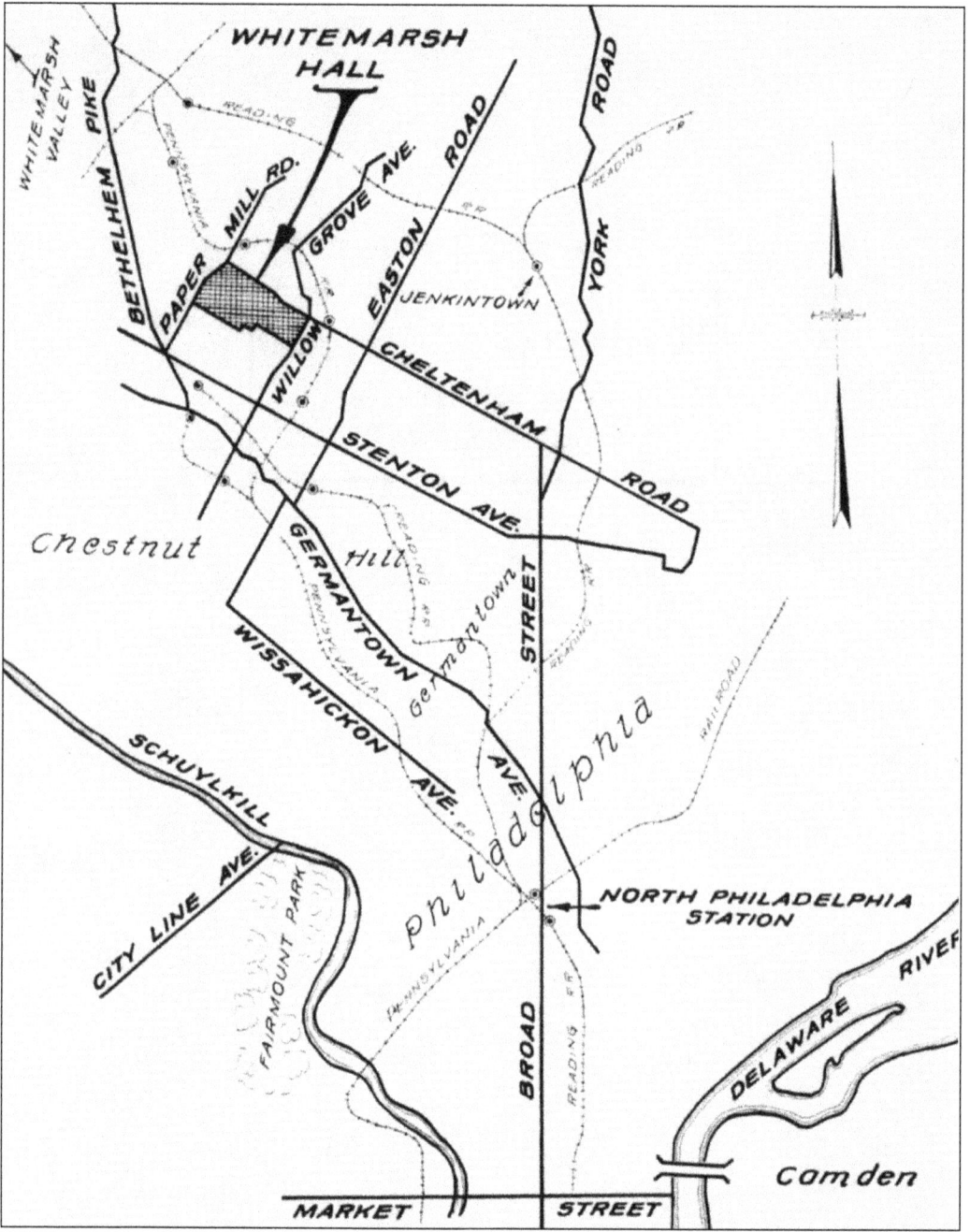

On June 9, 1915, Philadelphia newspapers reported that millionaire banker Edward Stotesbury had purchased a 200-acre tract of ground in Springfield Township, near Chestnut Hill. Stotesbury confessed that he intended to build a home there and, unbeknownst to the public, had already commissioned architects to begin designing what would become one of the largest houses in the country. Stotesbury was already familiar with Springfield, having established his horse farm in the Wyndmoor section in 1899. (Courtesy of ATOFINA Chemicals.)

IMAGES
of America

WHITEMARSH HALL
THE ESTATE OF
EDWARD T. STOTESBURY

Charles G. and Edward C. Zwicker
with the Springfield Township Historical Society

ARCADIA
PUBLISHING

Published by Arcadia Publishing
Charleston, South Carolina

Library of Congress Catalog Card Number: 2004104276

For all general information contact Arcadia Publishing at:
Telephone 843-853-2070
Fax 843-853-0044
E-mail sales@arcadiapublishing.com
For customer service and orders:
Toll-Free 1-888-313-2665

Visit us on the Internet at www.arcadiapublishing.com

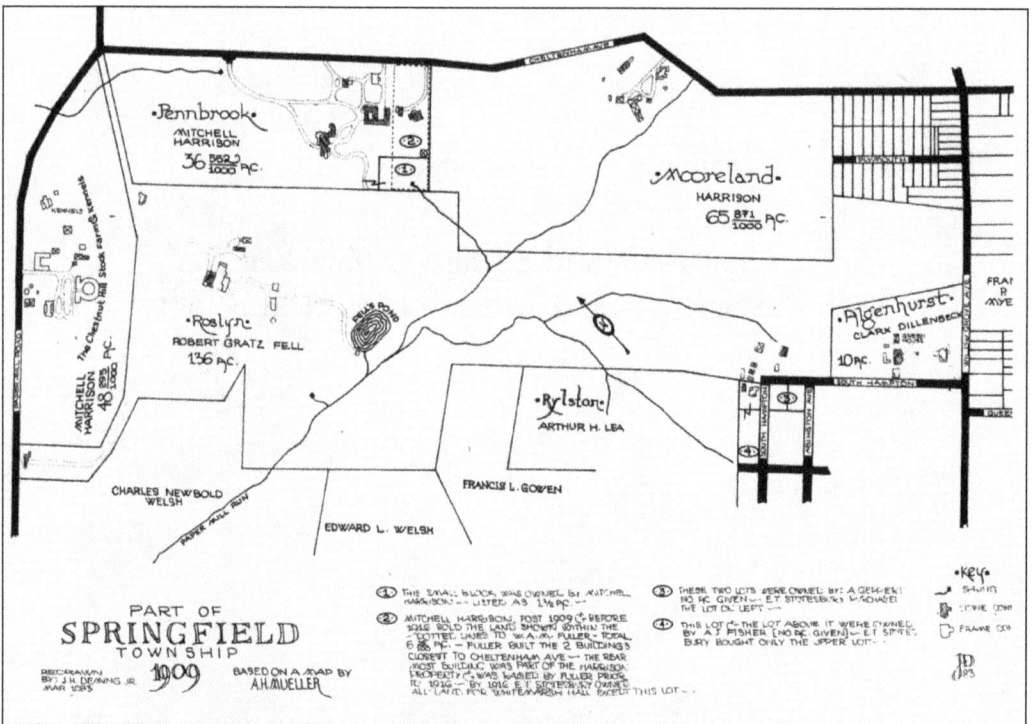

Edward Stotesbury had purchased the Robert Fell estate in Springfield Township. He also
acquired additional properties, including those of the Harrison and Dillenbeck families, to
extend his total estate to more than 300 acres. The Fell home was demolished to make way
for the new mansion, but many of the additional homes and structures on the property were
to remain. (Courtesy of John Deming.)

CONTENTS

PREFACE

The Springfield Township Historical Society was established in 1985, in large part as a result of the township and its interested residents losing battles to save significant historic buildings, including Whitemarsh Hall. A group of dedicated and energetic individuals founded the society, building it upon the precepts of research, education, and preservation.

Over the past two decades, the society's membership has grown tremendously, as have the results of the work done to support our mission. We have thoroughly documented—through deed research and photography—more than 100 of the township's oldest buildings. We hold presentations and programs, which are open to the public, four times a year on topics of local, regional, and worldwide interest. We conduct bus trips to historic locations in the tri-state area and beyond, for members and non-members. We have had all of our research papers, photographs, books, and memorabilia professionally organized and archived. In association with members of the community, we have worked to preserve historic landmarks in danger of being destroyed. Most recently, this included saving the Black Horse Inn, a 260-year-old tavern along a former stagecoach route running through Springfield Township.

A search continues to find a permanent home for the society, in which to house and display all of our valuable archives and to make them available for further education and research. The authors and the historical society thank you for your support in purchasing this book. We hope that you will enjoy reading it as much as we did in writing it. For further information, the group may be contacted by writing to the Springfield Township Historical Society, P.O. Box 564, Flourtown, PA 19031, or by calling (215) 233-4600.

—Charles G. Zwicker and Edward C. Zwicker IV,
on behalf of the Springfield Township Historical Society

INTRODUCTION

This book will focus on the great Philadelphia estate of Whitemarsh Hall and the life of its owner, Edward Townsend Stotesbury, one of the wealthiest Philadelphians in the early part of the 20th century. The reader will be given a glimpse into the magnificent era of the Gilded Age, when robber barons and industrialists built extravagant monuments to reflect their wealth and social position. Whitemarsh Hall was the ideal example of this era, considered by many to be architect Horace Trumbauer's residential masterpiece. Its memory and beauty will be reflected within these pages.

Edward Townsend Stotesbury, born in 1849, worked his way up through the ranks at Drexel & Company, from a $16-a-week clerk to a senior partner in the merged firm of Drexel & Company and J. P. Morgan & Company. At the peak of his wealth, Stotesbury was worth in excess of $100 million. In spite of this, he lived a relatively conservative lifestyle shared with his wife, Fannie Butcher, and their two daughters. Following Fannie's death shortly after giving birth to the second daughter, Edward raised the children. Once his daughters were grown and married, he traveled extensively for both business and pleasure. On one of these trips to Europe, he met, and was smitten with, Lucretia Roberts Cromwell. Eva, as her friends referred to her, was taking a break from nursing her dying husband and was attracted to Edward aboard ship. Their courtship resumed more intensely after her husband died; Edward and Eva were married in 1912. While Eva was used to traveling in the high society of Washington, Edward had been up to that point somewhat of a recluse, shunned from becoming a part of the Philadelphia elite. His second wife would show him how to spend his money to overcome this hurdle. Whitemarsh Hall would be his wedding present to her and their entrance key to Philadelphia's high society.

Stotesbury purchased several adjoining estates, totaling 300 acres, just north of Chestnut Hill, Philadelphia, in what is today known as Wyndmoor in Springfield Township. Groundbreaking commenced in October 1916, but the grand opening would not take place until five years later. It is estimated that construction of the house cost around $3 million and the interior decorating another $3 million to $5 million, excluding the artwork. The famous French landscape architect Jacques Greber designed the grounds and the English-style park atmosphere. Trumbauer's architectural designs for the home were principally Georgian in style. The mansion consisted of six levels (three above ground, three below), 147 rooms, 28 bathrooms, and 24 fireplaces in 100,000 square feet of floor space. The paintings, all original oils from famous European artists, were supplied by New York art and antiques dealer Joseph Duveen. Yearly maintenance on this property in its heyday was said to be $1 million. In spite of this, the Stotesburys lived there only in the spring and fall. They spent winters in Palm Beach, Florida, and summers in Bar Harbor, Maine.

The grand opening of Whitemarsh Hall was attended by 800 of Philadelphia's high society. The entertaining would continue for the next 17 years, and it was not uncommon to host as many as 600 guests at once. Stotesbury was renowned as one of the world's leading financiers at the time, and he kept company with United States presidents, European royalty, and powerful business figures.

The stock-market crash of 1929 and the subsequent Depression impacted even Stotesbury. It signaled a noticeable decline in the upkeep of the property. The outside staff was reduced, and the 300 manicured acres were turned to fields, except for the areas immediately around the house and driveway. Fear of a class uprising forced the Stotesburys to close Whitemarsh Hall in 1932 and to retreat to Europe for the year. Coupled with the Depression was the advent of the federal income tax, which would further deplete Stotesbury's bank account. By 1938, when Edward passed away, his net worth was estimated at $4 million. Although left with the lifetime use of Whitemarsh Hall, Eva was unable to afford it, so she put the house up for sale and moved.

The Pennsylvania Salt Manufacturing Company purchased the mansion and some of the surrounding acreage in 1943, and transformed the property for its headquarters and laboratories. Much of the remaining 300 acres was sold off to a developer who built post–World War II single-family homes as part of a development named Whitemarsh Village. When Pennsalt moved its operations to Valley Forge, Pennsylvania, in 1963, the mansion was left vacant. While it passed through a couple of subsequent owners, it became a target of arson and vandalism. Many ideas for Whitemarsh Hall's restoration were discussed throughout the years, but nothing ever came of it except a wrecking ball in 1980. Today, the 183-home Stotesbury Townhouse complex resides on the immediate mansion grounds. Remnants of the past glory include the 50-foot front columns that once held up the entranceway and portico, one of the Belvederes, the main gatehouse and towers, and some statuary. These remnants, people's memories, and this book will mark one of the great estates in this country: Whitemarsh Hall.

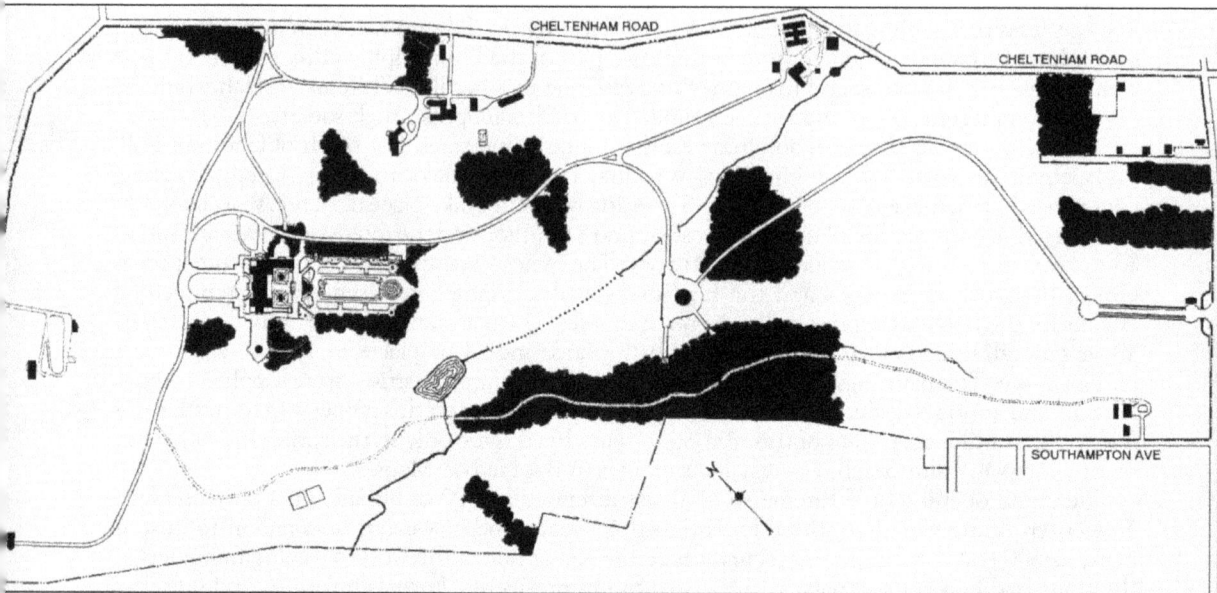

The mansion was to be built on top of a ridge looking out over the rolling hills of the Whitemarsh Valley. Cost would be no object in building a home that reflected the wealth and position of Edward Stotesbury. What was soon known as Whitemarsh Hall would become one of the grandest and most opulent homes of the 20th century. (Courtesy of E. C. Zwicker III.)

One

THE STOTESBURYS OF PHILADELPHIA

The man who would one day be known as "The Little King" was a Philadelphia boy who became one of the richest men in the country. Edward Townsend Stotesbury—investment banker, philanthropist, and multimillionaire—was once praised by J. P. Morgan as "knowing more about the banking business than any man in America." When this photograph was taken at the 1914 World Series in Philadelphia (with his second wife, Eva, and stepson Jimmy), E. T. was at the pinnacle of his wealth, with a personal fortune of more than $100 million. He was senior partner of one of the largest investment houses in the country, sat on the boards of numerous corporations and institutions, and was the friend of presidents and princes. This was the man who would build Whitemarsh Hall, "The Versailles of America."

Edward Stotesbury was born in Philadelphia on February 26, 1849. His father, Thomas (pictured here), was the third generation of the family in this country. Their ancestors had arrived from England via Ireland in the early 1700s. Thomas was a successful businessman; he owned a sugar refinery that he had started with money inherited from his father, a sea captain who had amassed a fortune in the molasses trade between Philadelphia and Jamaica in the 1800s.

While the business connections of his father launched young Edward on his financial career, the beliefs and values of his mother molded the man and established his moral foundation. Martha Stotesbury was from a well-known Philadelphia Quaker family. She named the oldest of her three boys after the prominent local Quaker Edward Townsend, although from an early age her son was nicknamed "Ned."

After attending the Friends Central School and Pierce Business College, Ned (pictured) was given a position with a wholesale grocery firm, from which he resigned after a few months in order to join the family business of Harris and Stotesbury. This position was also short-lived. Ned's father then secured him a position with the banking firm of Drexel & Company. At 17 years old, Ned started at Drexel, making just $200 per year.

On the first day of Ned's employment, Anthony Drexel, head of the firm and always the first to arrive, found young Stotesbury waiting for the business to open. Ned endeared himself to Drexel through his strong work ethic and ability to grasp the complex details of the financial world. This image shows the Drexel offices at 15th and Walnut Streets c. 1870. Prior to this time, the offices had been located at 5th and Chestnut Streets.

In April 1873, Stotesbury married Fannie Butcher, shown here with their daughter Edith. By 1875, he had been made junior partner at Drexel and was given a percentage of the firm's profits. Fannie, who did not understand the importance of this promotion, commented, "Edward, it would be far better if I saw more of thee, than all thy money." Crushed by her statement, Stotesbury never mentioned work to her again. (Courtesy of Cintra and Wayne Willcox.)

In 1878, Fannie gave birth to a daughter, Edith, and E. T. began construction on a summer home, Sulgrave (pictured), located on his parents' estate at Chelten Hills. Fannie and Edward's second daughter, Frances, arrived in November 1881. Fannie died shortly after the delivery from complications of childbirth. Devastated, Stotesbury secluded himself from the world. The family used Sulgrave as a summer home until 1890, when E. T. sold it to his brother-in-law.

In 1888, Stotesbury lost both of his parents. They were survived by Edward, his sister, and two brothers. Thomas left each of his sons $140,000. While Edward appreciated this gesture, he had already achieved financial success and independence. Thomas and Martha Stotesbury are buried—along with Edward, his first wife, Fannie, and their infant daughter Helen—at the Woodlands Cemetery in West Philadelphia. (Courtesy of Deborah C. Wilson.)

After Fannie's death, the Mt. Vernon Street home the Stotesburys had shared was sold, and E. T. moved with his daughters into the Aldine Hotel, located at 20th and Chestnut Streets. To ease his grief, Stotesbury immersed himself in work and began to travel abroad, taking an interest in collecting artwork. Always a lover of horses, he frequently drove a team of "Gentleman Roadsters" near his parents' estate.

In 1890, the family moved to 255 Tulpehocken Street in Germantown. By 1893, Stotesbury had become senior partner at Drexel; his wealth and reputation as a financial genius were secure. Over the next few years, he established relationships with Presidents McKinley, Roosevelt, Taft, and Coolidge. E. T. became active in numerous social clubs and civic associations (including the Union League), several cricket and country clubs, Radnor Hunt, and leagues in London and Paris.

Stotesbury purchased this Philadelphia property, at the northeast corner of 20th and Walnut Streets, in 1899. The mansion had been designed by noted Philadelphia architect Frank Furness. This home provided a suitable setting for business, entertaining, and an increasing collection of fine artwork Stotesbury acquired while traveling abroad. In 1910, he purchased the adjoining townhouse from the McKean family and, having no need for the quarters himself, leased the property to others.

The Grand Ballroom was later redesigned in the style of Louis XIV as part of a major expansion and renovation project, managed by E. T.'s second wife, at an estimated cost of $1.5 million to $2 million. The mansion and adjoining townhouse were combined to provide space for entertaining and additional living quarters. The architect and decorators who worked on this renovation project were later commissioned by the Stotesburys to design Whitemarsh Hall.

In 1899, Stotesbury purchased 40 acres at East and Mermaid Lanes in Springfield Township. His Winoga Stock Farm was named after his favorite mare and principal prize winner. The farm raised and trained numerous trotters that competed in shows all over the world. Believing it extravagant to maintain his stable during World War I, Stotesbury sold his horses in 1918 and converted the farm to food production.

This trophy was one of many won by Stotesbury's trotters. E. T. was a major organizer of the Philadelphia Horse Show, held annually in Chestnut Hill across from the Wissahickon Inn, a popular summer resort that is now the Chestnut Hill Academy. What was once the show grounds are now part of the Philadelphia Cricket Club. (Courtesy of Dan Helwig.)

Edward and Fannie's daughters grew into beautiful women and were an asset to their father through his years as a widower. Edith was closest to her father, often traveling with him on business trips to Europe. She married Sydney Emlen Hutchinson, a well-known Philadelphia insurance broker, and had three children. When she died suddenly in the spring of 1935, E. T. was devastated, and the family went into mourning for almost a year.

16

Frances Stotesbury married John Kearsley Mitchell III in 1909 and they had two children. Mitchell was the president of the Philadelphia Rubber Works and a prominent man in Philadelphia. When Mitchell's mistress was murdered in 1923, rumors abounded that Stotesbury had paid out more than $1 million to quiet any speculation of his son-in-law's involvement. Frances remained married to Mitchell even after the scandal. She died in October 1950. (Courtesy of Richard C. Marchand.)

The 54-year-old Edward Stotesbury appears at the pinnacle of his career. He was a multimillionaire, one of the most powerful men in the country, and a major figure in world finance. In an era when the average life expectancy was 47 years old, E. T. had reason to look back at his life and be proud of his achievements. But it would be the second half of his life that would bring Stotesbury notoriety. (Courtesy of Craig Seltzer.)

Stotesbury was 60 years old when he met Lucretia Roberts Cromwell, seen here in a bridal gown at her first wedding in 1889. She and E. T. had met on a cruise to Europe shortly before her husband passed away in 1909. For Stotesbury, it was love at first sight; they married on January 18, 1912. His gifts to her included a reported $4 million in cash, a $100,000 sapphire necklace, and jewelry that once belonged to Queen Isabella of Spain.

It was said that after the death of his first wife, Stotesbury was heartbroken at having always saved their money instead of enjoying his wealth with Fannie. This was not to happen with his second marriage. He would deny Eva nothing, and eventually spent more than $50 million on her. As a belated wedding present, in 1915 E. T. purchased a 200-acre tract near Chestnut Hill for $250,000. He commissioned Philadelphia architect Horace Trumbauer to begin designs for what would be one of the largest houses ever built in the United States. The era of Whitemarsh Hall was about to begin.

Two

THE BEGINNING
OF AN ERA

Edward Stotesbury considered several suburban locations for his new estate, but decided upon the Wyndmoor section of Springfield Township, overlooking the Whitemarsh Valley. He purchased five separate estates, totaling approximately 300 acres, a mile from his Winoga Stock Farm. On October 20, 1916, the George A. Fuller Company broke ground on what would be a five-year construction project. In this photograph, taken on February 14, 1917, the east side of the mansion's foundation is built. Two sub-basements were created under this part of the house. The lowest level housed the boilers and coal bins, while the next level consisted of additional wood and coal bins, a vegetable cellar, the servants' trunk room, and additional storage. Opening to the outside only on the west wing, the ground floor included the servants' kitchen and dining room, the shipping and receiving area, the main kitchen, the wine cellar, a movie theater, a men's locker room, and gentlemen's and ladies' wardrobes.

Horace Trumbauer (1868–1938) was not formally educated as an architect, but he served a six-year apprenticeship in the firm of G. W. and W. D. Hewitt before striking out on his own. For his chief designer, he hired Julian Abele, the first African-American graduate of the University of Pennsylvania's School of Architecture. Whitemarsh Hall's design, a collaborative effort of the two men, was considered Trumbauer's most elaborate residential commission. (Courtesy of Craig Seltzer.)

Trumbauer was no stranger to Stotesbury, as the designer had previously remodeled Edward's Walnut Street mansion. Given Whitemarsh Hall's extensive requirement of 147 rooms and 100,000 square feet of floor space, Trumbauer used multiple basements and a concealed third floor so the house did not excessively spread out above ground and appear grotesque. Though rarely photographed, Trumbauer (far right) is shown here at the construction site with, from left to right, Edward, Eva, and Eva's son, Jimmy Cromwell. (Courtesy of Free Library of Philadelphia.)

In this photograph, taken on January 14, 1917, the walls have been erected for the first floor of the mansion. The wing to the right is the completed entranceway to the Tea Room, or West Loggia. The section on the left is the northwest corner of the front of the house, containing Eva's library. Walls were erected here first because only one subfloor would be built under this section, with the more extensive excavation on the east side still under way.

By August 22, 1917, the front facing of the house had been completed, and the columns were stacked in pieces on the lawn, waiting to be assembled as part of the Georgian entranceway. Below the first-floor windows, the air intakes into the cellar are visible before being covered with grates. In the distance is Whitemarsh Lodge, where Eva lived during the construction of the mansion. It was torn down upon the mansion's completion.

Three months after the previous scene, on November 21, 1917, the 50-foot-high Ionic columns were in place, with the third-floor portico still under construction. Note the boiler for the steam-powered engine that was used to hoist the heavy building materials into place. At the far right is one of many temporary work sheds that dotted the property during the construction period.

Horace Trumbauer poses in the completed entranceway between the first and second pillars on February 27, 1918. The walkways leading up to the front door are still under construction. Note the round porthole window in the portico—this was the only third-floor bedroom window that could be seen from the outside. The window was in the bedroom of Henry Spragg, E. T.'s English valet. All the other third-floor windows were hidden behind the balustrade encircling the Rooftop Terrace.

In 1917, Eva wrote a letter to Trumbauer stating, in part, "I have never been able to find an expression in words for the majestic simplicity and beauty of the new house which is so satisfying, so thrilling in its loveliness that it sometimes brings tears to my eyes when I see it at sunset or in the moonlight."

This December 1, 1919 photograph was likely taken from the Portico Guest Suite's small bedroom. The view looks down on the front driveway just to the side of the columns holding up the portico. The two buildings whose rooftops can be seen beyond the driveway are likely structures belonging to previous owner Mitchell Harrison that were eventually torn down. In the distance is the Whitemarsh Valley, where the Erdenheim and Flourtown areas of Springfield Township would be built.

The temporary rooftop storage structures built a year earlier had been removed by the time this photograph was taken on April 18, 1919. Here, the outer structure is near completion. The main part of the house was 283 feet wide by 100 feet deep. As part of landscape architect Jacques Greber's original symmetrical landscape design, there was an east-side garden that came off the Summer (or East) Loggia, which was later removed.

The side entrance to the Summer Loggia bears a striking similarity to the entranceway of Stotesbury's Walnut Street mansion. In this photograph, taken March 18, 1918, the adjoining fountain and handrail structures are still covered with wood to protect them from the continuing construction activity around the mansion.

Located on the east side of the mansion, the service entrance for pickups and deliveries is seen here on February 26, 1919. This area was accessible via a road off Cheltenham Avenue; the gates are pictured on page 122. The cobblestoned courtyard was considered the mansion's ground floor, as described earlier. The two floors seen above this 83- by 33-foot mezzanine contained servants' bedrooms and the butler's and housekeeper's offices.

A crane lifts doorframes into place on the east side's closed-in Belvedere, which was known as the Orangerie. The roof of this entire wing provided a walking terrace off the Valley and Terrace Suites reserved for Eva's children, Jimmy and Louise. This photograph was taken on June 13, 1917.

Major excavation work is under way on April 30, 1918. Workers dig out the hillside to accommodate the garden retaining wall to the right and the formal gardens to the left. The exterior house construction is fairly complete. Now the focus is on the outside plantings and the interior finishing work.

Since Stotesbury served as president of the Reading Railroad Company, it was logical that a spur would be built out to the construction site. Trains arrived almost daily, loaded with sand, cement, stone, granite, marble, and steel. Hundreds of tons of concrete were mixed in a small plant that had been erected on the premises. The mansion's exterior surface was finished with a covering of Indiana limestone.

Steel beams, similar to those used today to support highway overpasses, were laid in place to form the foundation of the mansion. In this photograph, taken on June 20, 1917, the steam-powered cranes lift building materials into place. Construction on the third floor is beginning and, when finished, will be topped with a copper roof and hidden rain gutters and downspouts.

This reflecting pool, 90 feet in diameter, anchored the end of the formal gardens. Beneath it is a room filled with pipes, shutoff valves, and switches that controlled water flow to the lead fountains (yet to be installed above). This photograph was taken on July 12, 1919. Just a year earlier, E. T. had redirected the builder's steam shovels to the nearby Holy Sepulcher Cemetery to assist in the burial of influenza victims.

The final construction phase of the Grotto, which is recessed into the retaining wall, is shown here on February 26, 1919. Statuary of Neptune and an accompanying female figure would be added later as the final touch. The figures will hold a large urn that will continuously spill water out into the pond just in front of the Grotto itself.

Construction proceeded year round, as this December 26, 1917 photograph indicates. Here, workers build the back Terrace, where many parties would be held. As a reference, the door on the far left is the main entrance into the middle of the Ballroom. The worker in the middle of this image, kneeling down, uses a modified wheelbarrow to move pre-poured concrete sections into place.

Jacques Greber came to the United States in 1910 to design gardens for Clarence H. Mackay's Harbor Hill estate on Long Island and for P. A. B. Widener's Lynnewood Hall. Enlisted by Trumbauer to create the gardens for Whitemarsh Hall, Greber included statuary carved by his father, sculptor Henri-Léon Greber, in the garden plan. Excellent examples of the French classical design, these gardens were intended to be an extension to the mansion.

Greber used twine to outline his design for the gardens of the Upper Terrace, just off the back of the house. His designs, like Trumbauer's plans for the house itself, were symmetrically laid out, featuring two reflecting pools, one on each side of the Terrace, both surrounded by plantings. This photograph was taken on March 19, 1919.

Greber's designs come to life here, on August 20, 1919. The gardens sloped slightly downward, so they could be seen by people entering the main gates on Willow Grove Avenue. White gravel was used on the footpaths as well as on the winding two-mile driveway leading up to the mansion. This view looks south toward Willow Grove Avenue, where the main gatehouse stands at the top of the rise, one mile away. Note that the garden retaining wall along the left side is now completed, along with the planting of all of the trees constituting Maple Alley. Workers can be seen in the far end of the gardens, by the reflecting pools, doing the initial grading for the Plaza.

On May 2, 1919, workers pull a tree erect during the creation of Maple Alley, which ran along the ridge above the retaining wall on the east side of the lower gardens. Each of these large maples was brought individually by flatbed truck up Philadelphia's Broad Street to the mansion. E. T. was 72 years old when Whitemarsh Hall was completed, so there was no time to wait for saplings to grow into mature trees.

The southwest, back side of the mansion is revealed here. The Tea Room extends out on the left side, with Eva's Terrace above it. Just to the right of that is the Drawing Room, with Eva's boudoir and the Empire Loggia above. The door and windows of the Ballroom and the windows of the Breakfast Room are seen at the back of the house. The Dining Room is still under construction in this May 16, 1917 photograph.

Construction of the house and property required many different types of machinery and transportation. Here, a horse-drawn wagon is in use while the Belvedere undergoes its final phases of construction. Enlargement of the photograph shows the following on the front of the wagon on the right: "J. Winn 304 N. 39th St." This photograph was taken on October 31, 1917.

With this October 3, 1917 photograph of the Tea Room entrance, and the following image of the Shady Garden just off it, this chapter has come full circle around the exterior of the house during its various phases of construction. While the majority of the outside shell of the house was erected in about a year's time, the required interior finishing work would delay the grand opening.

The Shady Garden, situated on the western side of the mansion, is under construction on April 2, 1919. The garden provided a particularly lovely view from the Rooftop Terrace off Eva's Bedroom. When finished, the Shady Garden would include white-gravel walking paths and sitting benches under the shade trees, where one could enjoy the serenity of the large reflecting pool.

Building the estate's access roads, including the two-mile road that stretched from the main entrance at Willow Grove Avenue to the mansion, was backbreaking work. William J. Winning Sr. was one of those workers who simply used a pick and a shovel to dig the first roads on the property. He recalled earning wages of $18.90 for a six-day workweek, working from 8 a.m. until 4:30 p.m. each day. This photograph was taken on September 5, 1919.

By October 18, 1919, when this photograph was taken, the Plaza had taken shape. It would be derisively referred to as "the Fried Egg" because of its appearance from above, but never in the presence of the Stotesburys. At this juncture, the statuary and accompanying balustrades remain to be added to complete the final effect. The original design called for the addition of a large pool with multiple fountains, but this was never included.

While the mansion's exterior was near completion, the main entrance and gatehouse on Willow Grove Avenue were under construction (pictured here). Stotesbury purchased and razed several homes along Willow Grove and Cheltenham Avenues, including the Clark Dillenbeck home (called Algenhurst), on the corner of Willow Grove and Southampton Avenues. The materials from this demolished house were donated for the construction of the Seven Dolors School across the street. This photograph was taken on October 18, 1919.

A worker takes a break from creating the interior work for the Entrance Hall, sometime in late 1919. Interior designer Sir Charles Carrick Allom planned the principal first-floor rooms, as well as the second-floor bedrooms and hallways, in the Georgian style. Edouard Hitau of Alavoine, France, was brought in to create the French-style rooms Eva desired, including the first-floor Reception Room and some of Eva's personal second-floor suites.

The interior finishing work was delayed due to World War I restrictions and the difficulty in obtaining materials from Europe. After the armistice signing in 1918, the final designs were implemented. This photograph of the Ballroom's east-end construction was taken on August 20, 1919. Trap doors were installed in closets and hallways to allow access above the foot-thick plaster ceilings and the bank of pipes and electrical wiring within them.

The Billiard Room, here under construction on August 20, 1919, was destined to be the exclusive territory of the gentlemen, with their after-dinner cigars and brandy. The doorway on the far left led to the East Rotunda and the one on the right led to the Men's Room. This window on the right looked out on the front portico and entrance steps.

This view looks down the second-floor hallway, toward the Stotesburys' living quarters, on August 20, 1919. A skylight can be seen just in front of the doorway to the Portico Guest Suite's secondary, small bedroom. Immediately to the right of the foreground columns is the stairway leading down to the Entrance Hall. Just over two years later, the finishing work was completed, the furnishings in place, and the Stotesburys in residence and ready for the grand opening of Whitemarsh Hall. Sadly, on June 25, 1920, Eva's father, Judge James Henry Roberts, passed away while visiting the grand estate.

36

Three

IN ITS HEYDAY

Whitemarsh Hall opened to the public on October 8, 1921. The event was used as an occasion to introduce Delphine Dodge, Jimmy's Cromwell's bride, to Philadelphia society. After four years of construction, at a cost of $3 million to $5 million, Whitemarsh Hall was celebrated with a formal housewarming party for more than 800 guests. Trains were chartered to bring the guests from the city. The Philadelphia Rapid Transit Company, of which Stotesbury was director, sent buses to convey guests down Willow Grove Avenue, through the main gates, and into the estate. This early photograph of the main gates does not show the ornate urns that were placed on top of each pillar shortly after construction was completed.

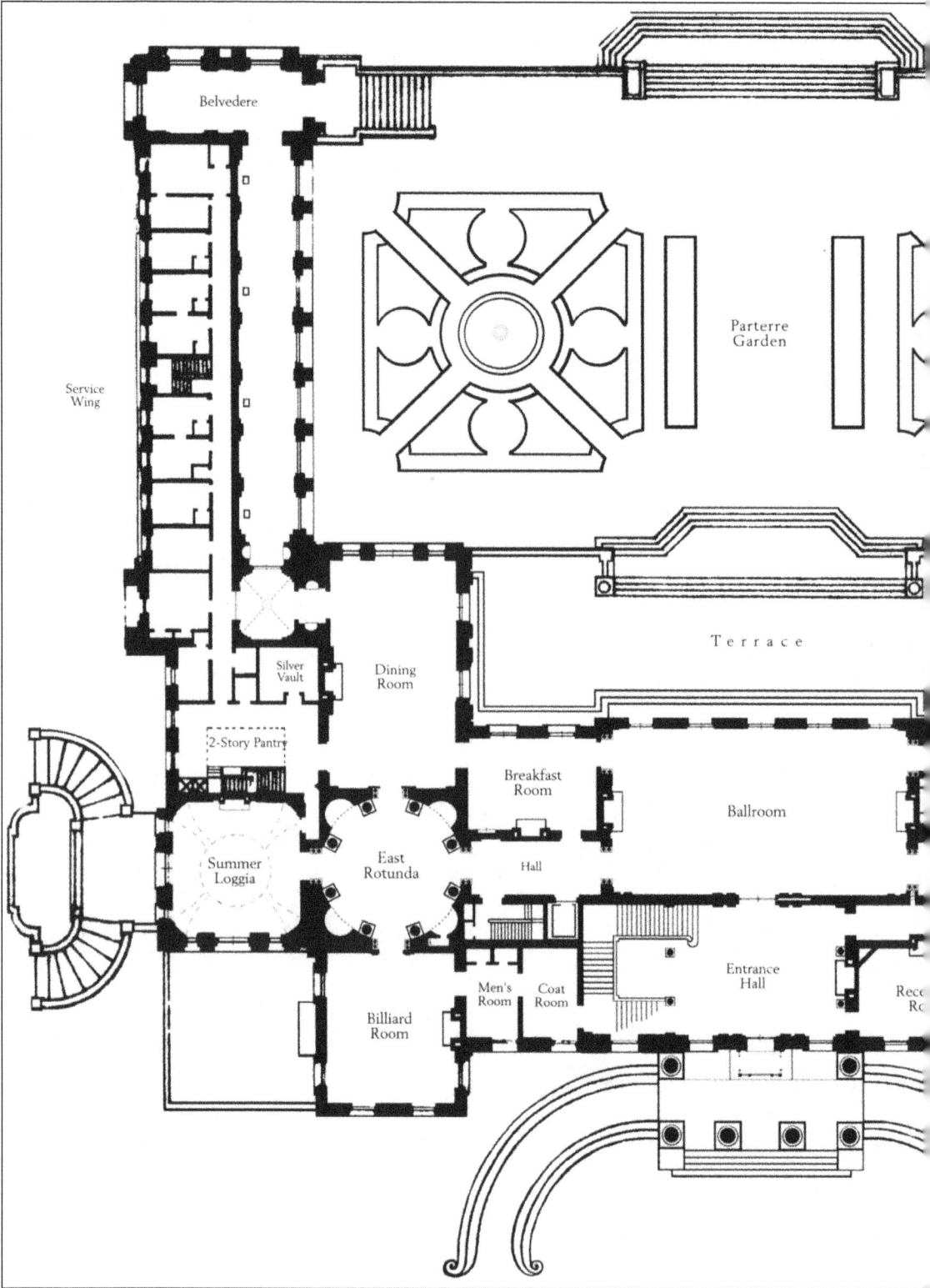

Belvedere

Service
Wing

Parterre
Garden

T e r r a c e

Silver
Vault

Dining
Room

2-Story Pantry

Breakfast
Room

Ballroom

Summer
Loggia

East
Rotunda

Hall

Billiard
Room

Men's
Room

Coat
Room

Entrance
Hall

Rece
Ro

Drawing
Room

Terrace

mall
brary

West
Rotunda

Tea
Room

an Hall

Ladies
Room

Mrs. S's
Library

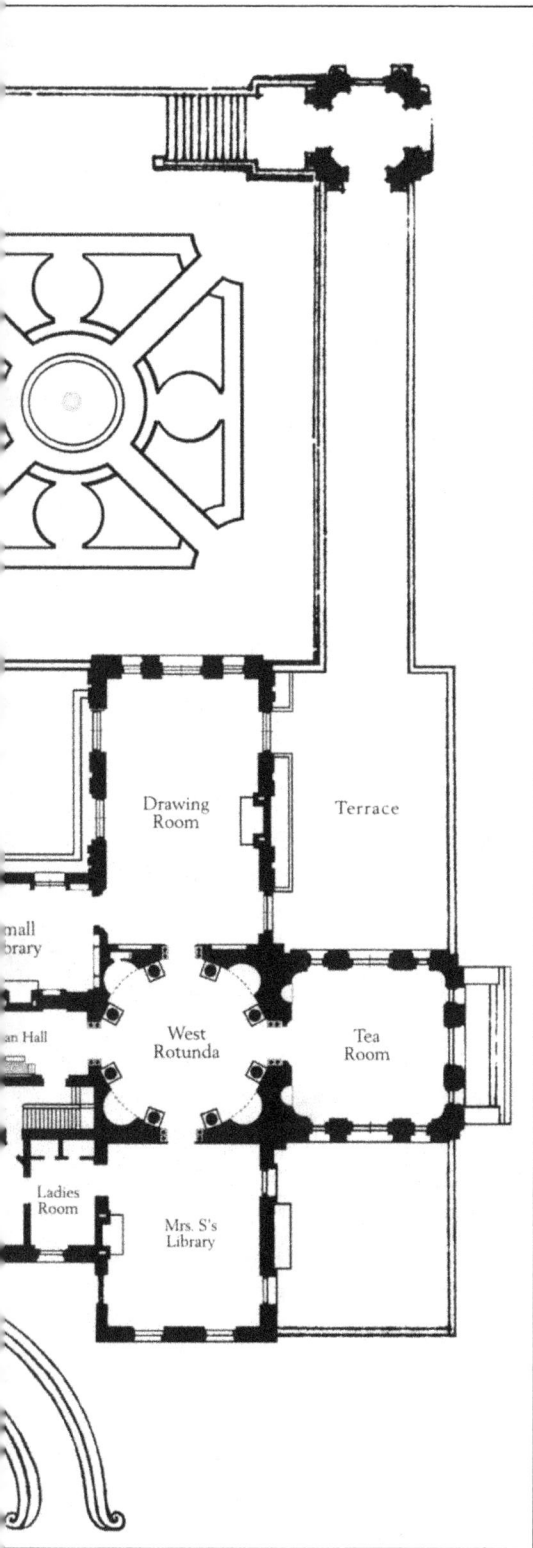

The first-floor plan is seen here. These two pages, along with the following two, show blueprints of the first and second floors for reference while touring the mansion in this chapter. (Courtesy of Richard C. Marchand.)

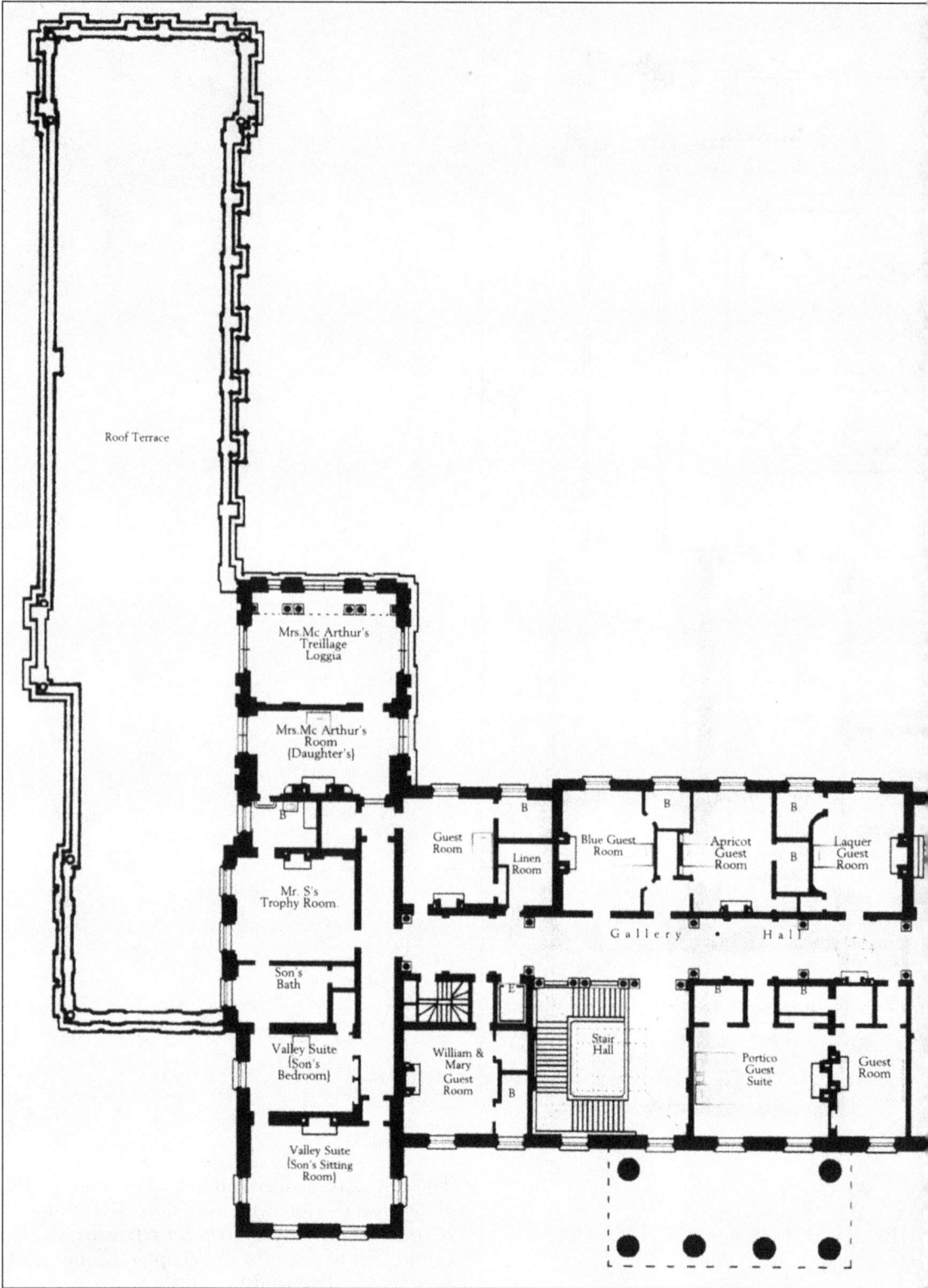

Roof Terrace

Mrs. McArthur's
Treillage
Loggia

Mrs. McArthur's
Room
{Daughter's}

B

Mr. S's
Trophy Room.

Son's
Bath

Valley Suite
{Son's
Bedroom}

Valley Suite
{Son's Sitting
Room}

Guest
Room

Linen
Room

B

B

Blue Guest
Room

Apricot
Guest
Room

B

Laquer
Guest
Room

B

Gallery • Hall

E

B

William &
Mary
Guest
Room

B

Stair
Hall

B

B

Portico
Guest
Suite

Guest
Room

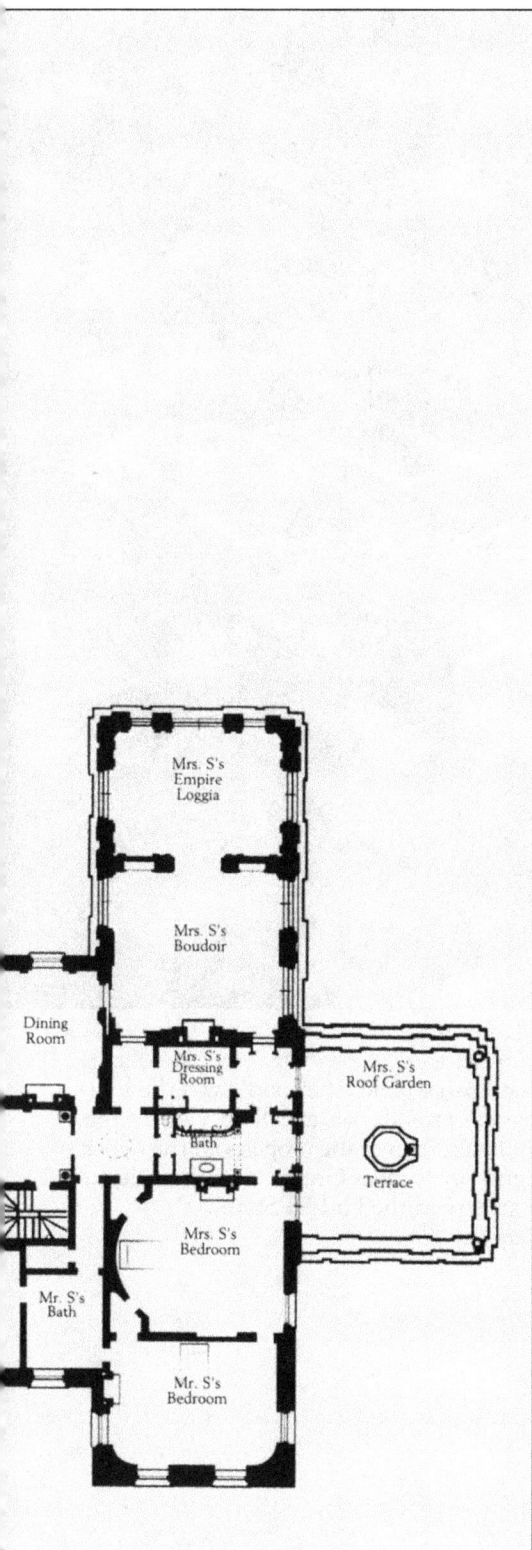

Mrs. S's
Empire
Loggia

Mrs. S's
Boudoir

Dining
Room

Mrs. S's
Dressing
Room

Mrs. S's
Roof Garden

Bath

Terrace

Mrs. S's
Bedroom

Mr. S's
Bath

Mr. S's
Bedroom

This is the plan for the second floor. The room names on this diagram and the preceding one correspond with the descriptions in this chapter. Starting in the Entrance Hall on the first floor, the tour will proceed from the west side of the mansion to the east. (Courtesy of Richard C. Marchand.)

Visitors were awed by the magnificence and scale of the estate. From the main gates, one would proceed along a mile-long road that ran past formal gardens, statuary, and woodland. Approaching the mansion from the back, the road wound past Maple Alley and down the long driveway to the front of the house. This aerial photograph provides an excellent view of the estate, with Cheltenham Avenue defining the northern boundaries of the property in the upper part of the photograph. The grounds and gardens, designed by Jacques Greber, were considered to be the finest example of French classical landscape artistry in the United States.

This aerial photograph of the back of the mansion provides a bird's-eye view of the formal gardens. As mentioned earlier, these back gardens were laid out on a slightly declined angle so they could be seen as one entered the estate from Willow Grove Avenue, a mile away. Referred to as a *tapis vert* (green carpet of turf), this garden measured 500 feet by 250 feet.

From the time the mansion opened in 1921 until the Depression years starting in 1929, the Stotesburys would entertain lavishly, often hosting parties for more than 600 people. Princes and presidents, cardinals and generals accepted invitations to these events. Here, Mr. and Mrs. Stotesbury (on right) entertain Will Rogers (second from left) and Jimmy Cromwell. Rogers was not invited back after he joked that the wine tasted like flat ginger ale.

The estate's 300 acres extended from Willow Grove Avenue on the east to Paper Mill Road on the west, and from Cheltenham Avenue at its northern edge to Southampton Avenue at the south. More than 70 gardeners were employed to maintain the grounds, operating 20 lawn mowers, 8 tractors, and about a dozen power mowers. During World War I, Johnny Boyd, a great-uncle of the authors, was hired to cut the grass with his team of horses. The estate had four large greenhouses for growing and maintaining various trees and ferns. Additional greenhouses, located off Southampton Avenue, provided all the cut flowers for the mansion. The boxwood shrubs planted along Willow Grove Avenue came from George Washington's Mt. Vernon home. Stotesbury once said that it cost him more than $1 million per year to maintain the house and property.

E. T. stands in front of the mansion's main entrance in 1928, shortly after recovering from a near-fatal car accident. The Stotesburys lived in Palm Beach, Florida, from mid-January to late April; resided at Whitemarsh Hall from April until July; and summered at Bar Harbor, Maine, from July until September. The couple then returned to Philadelphia to close out the year. Their schedule also included about six weeks in Europe each spring. (Courtesy of Temple University Urban Archives.)

Trumbauer designed Whitemarsh Hall in the French neoclassical style of Versailles Palace. Indiana limestone and Italian marble were used to construct the 100,000-square-foot mansion, which had 147 rooms, 28 bathrooms, and 3 elevators on 6 floors. The design also provided for a 5,000-square-foot kitchen, a movie theater, a gymnasium, a wine cellar, tennis courts, and a 64-foot-long Ballroom with two marble fireplaces imported from Italy at a cost of more than $60,000 each.

46

Sir Charles Carrick Allom was knighted for his work as the decorator of both Buckingham and Windsor Palaces during the reign of King George V. Allom worked closely on many projects with art dealer Joseph Duveen in both Great Britain and America. Duveen was the one who recommended Allom to Eva Stotesbury. Allom's conception for Whitemarsh Hall provided for a Georgian palace design with both classical French and English interiors.

Joseph Duveen was an English art dealer who built a business empire by selling art to the rich. He was influential in forming the collections of William Randolph Hearst, Andrew Mellon, John D. Rockefeller, and Joseph E. Widener. Likely introduced to Stotesbury by the Wideners, Duveen was commissioned to provide original works of art and all the furnishings for the mansion. Duveen truly provided the vision behind Whitemarsh Hall, since it was he who recommended Horace Trumbauer as architect, Jacques Greber as landscape designer, and Charles Carrick Allom as decorator.

When entering the mansion, one passed through the foyer into the Entrance Hall. The statuary seen in this photograph, *The Sacrifice of the Arrows of Love on the Altar of Friendship* by Jean Pierre Tassart, was once owned by Frederick the Great. Ionic columns divided the foyer from the stairwell, which rose up through two stories to an attic skylight. Lighting for this room was also provided by an enormous crystal chandelier.

On the right side of the Entrance Hall was a marble fireplace, over which hung a portrait of Edward Stotesbury painted by R. L. Partington. The table was from the Louis XIV period. Chinese porcelain temple jars on either side of the Ballroom entrance were from the Yung Cheng period. The arched doorway leading into the Ballroom held a sliding pocket door that could be moved into the wall during parties and large gatherings.

Immediately off the right side of the Entrance Hall was the Reception Room. This room was designed to highlight a series of eight Louis XIV painted panels designed by Edouard Hitau of Alavoine, France. On the mantle is an 18th-century bust once owned by the Countess of Carnarvon. A Louis XV roll-top desk is prominently displayed on the far wall.

From the Reception Room, one passed through the Ladies' Room to reach Mrs. Stotesbury's Library (pictured). It was from this room that Eva managed three estates, hundreds of servants, and an impressive social schedule that included volunteer and charitable events. Her managerial and organizational skills would have put most corporate executives to shame. The portrait on the right side is *Mrs. Andrew Hay* by Sir Henry Raeburn. The double doors to the right of the desk led to the West Rotunda.

The West Rotunda was one of two matching rooms on either side of the Ballroom. Here, the Stotesburys displayed famous statuary and sculptures. Seen here at center is one of a famous pair of works by French sculptor Clodion that were brought from Paris in 1922 and purchased for $70,000. It was said that one could whisper a sentence in one Rotunda and be heard across the Ballroom in the opposite Rotunda, a distance of more than 120 feet.

Connected to the West Rotunda was an enclosed Loggia, known as the Tea Room, that served as a tropical sunroom. Because of Whitemarsh Hall's symmetrical design, there were matching Loggias, Rotundas, and Terraces on either side of the mansion. Each Loggia measured 32 feet square. It was here in the Tea Room that Cardinal Mercer blessed the house on October 8, 1921. A plaque was placed on the floor to commemorate the event.

Moving in from the Tea Room and back through the Rotunda, one entered the Drawing Room from the right side of this photograph. Decorated in French Provincial style, the room was also referred to as the White and Gold Room. The portrait over the fireplace, entitled *Lady Elizabeth Conyngham*, was painted by Sir Thomas Lawrence. Elizabeth was the sister of Lady Maria Conyngham, whose portrait hung in Mr. Stotesbury's library.

Mr. Stotesbury's library, referred to as the Small Library, was located between the Drawing Room and the Ballroom and was decorated with dark paneling and a coffered ceiling. E. T. was a collector of antique clocks, examples of which could usually be seen on the mantle or his desk. The room was filled with leather-bound volumes and first editions; however, Stotesbury rarely read books, preferring instead to gain his knowledge through experience.

The Organ Hall, located on the west side of the house, served as a walkway between the Rotunda and the Ballroom. This hall also contained an elevator to the Stotesburys' living quarters and the third floor. The house had nine elevators—three for residential use and the remainder for carrying freight or use as dumbwaiters.

Eva had insisted on having a pipe organ in the Ballroom. Trumbauer refused to build it into his plans, but after Eva "ordered" him to find a location for it, the organ was placed in what became known as the Organ Hall. On Whitemarsh Hall's opening night, the organ was played by Frederick Taft of New York. Recitals were performed on most days, and E. T. gave standing orders that "The End of a Perfect Day" be played upon his arrival home from work in Philadelphia.

From the Organ Hall, one proceeded into the Ballroom. Perhaps the most impressive room in the mansion, it was 66 feet long by 35 feet wide. The polished inlaid hardwood floors were highlighted by two large marble fireplaces on either end of the room. Crystal chandeliers and a 53-foot Isfahan carpet added to the elegance.

This eastward view of the Ballroom reveals a portrait over the fireplace painted by Romney in 1788. Seventeenth-century French tapestries hang from the walls. Chinese porcelain temple jars from the Yung Cheng period adorn the tables. The Isfahan carpet, purchased by the Stotesburys for $90,000, was rolled up prior to parties and other events. In 1944, when Eva auctioned off the contents of the house after E. T.'s death, the carpet fetched a mere $5,000.

In addition to the Main Dining Room, the Stotesburys used the Breakfast Room as a dining area for daily meals and more intimate gatherings. Although most of the displayed artworks in the mansion were originals collected by Stotesbury over the years, many of the furniture pieces were reproductions. A number of the ornate moldings over the doors and fireplaces were fabricated from plaster, which was cheaper to use than wood.

During large dinner parties, guests sat here in the Dining Room, located at the back of the east wing of the mansion. This room was 68 feet by 28 feet, the same dimensions as the Drawing Room. The fireplace mantle of sculptured marble was inlaid with Sienna and Vert des Alpes marbles. Over the fireplace is the famous portrait of *Lady Lemon*, painted by George Romney in 1788.

54

For the first year after the mansion was opened, the Stotesburys borrowed from Joseph Duveen a statue of Diana (pictured here) until the famous pair of Clodion sculptures arrived from Paris. Diana was placed in the East Rotunda, which provided a straight-line view through the Great Hall to the West Rotunda. The sculptures by Clodion once decorated the elegant dining room of an 18th-century Paris home.

The two Loggias were designed with common elements in flooring, lighting, and furnishings, but the East (or Summer) Loggia provided a more austere feeling with its high marble walls and vaulted ceiling. Each morning, two men from Stotesbury's greenhouses would go to the mansion to inspect the indoor plants, watering them and replacing them as needed. Fresh-cut flowers from the greenhouses were brought into the mansion daily.

The Billiard Room was equipped with a pool table, card tables, and a slot machine. The room also provided a display area for E. T.'s collection of ribbons and trophies won by his famous trotters. In this room, men would congregate to talk of politics and finance, seeking advice and favor from the master of the house.

The Gallery Hall on the second floor ran the length of the main block of the mansion, directly above the Great Hall on the first floor. This hall provided access to the east and west bedroom suites and various guest rooms. While in residence at Whitemarsh Hall, the Stotesburys entertained constantly, with guests, children, and grandchildren often staying at the mansion for extended periods.

Proceeding west down the hallway, one first entered the Portico Guest Suite, whose windows looked out from under the front portico of the mansion. The guest rooms and suites were decorated in a mixture of styles and period designs. Four guest suites were located along the Back Terrace side of the house, while three others were located on the front side, overlooking the Whitemarsh Valley. These guest accommodations were in addition to the rooms and suites on the east wing that were used mainly for family.

In the Portico Suite, this small guest room adjoined the main suite. Each set of rooms was furnished in a different period or décor, and each guest suite had a private bathroom. In addition, each suite had its own stationery, a call button for the maids, and an assigned chauffeur.

Mr. Stotesbury's Bedroom was austere in its design, reflecting his Quaker upbringing. Featuring French prints from his art collection, the room offered a view looking north over the Whitemarsh Valley. His closet contained more than 100 pairs of shoes and 150 suits. Horace Lippincott, Stotesbury's biographer, described E. T. as "a small man with a fine handsome head set well upon his shoulders. His spare body was always scrupulously attired." He was often voted one of the best-dressed men in the country.

Mrs. Stotesbury's Suite, by contrast, was the most lavish set of rooms on the second floor. The Bedroom and adjoining suite were decorated in French Provincial style, using materials of marble, bronze, gold, and parquetry. The recessed alcove behind the bed was later removed to provide for a larger hallway access behind this wall and leading into the bedroom suites.

In Eva's Bedroom, a door to the left of the sofa provided entry to E. T.'s room. Doors on either side of her bed led to a back hallway that allowed access to both E. T.'s room and the Gallery Hall. Mrs. Stotesbury's Bedroom and Boudoir were designed by Charles Carrick Allom, while the rest of the Suite was designed by Edouard Hitau, who also created the Reception Room and both second-floor Loggias, pictured previously.

Eva's Roof Garden and Terrace looked out on the Shady Garden on the west side of the mansion and offered a spectacular view of the Whitemarsh Valley. The Terrace, above the first-floor Tea Room, provided Eva a private outdoor retreat. Here, she installed one of the first-ever automatic retractable awnings to provide shade and privacy.

Mrs. Stotesbury's Bath was a conversation piece for visitors to Whitemarsh Hall. It had an Italian marble bathtub and sink with solid-gold faucets. Eva often commented that the gold faucets, installed in her homes and private rail car, were less expensive than silver because they required less polishing.

Located directly off the Bathroom was Mrs. Stotesbury's Dressing Room. Eva was always the picture of fashion and she was proud of her system for maintaining an orderly wardrobe. On her staff was an artist who was responsible for drawing sketches of all Eva's dresses and gowns, which were then numbered and filed. Every day, Mrs. Stotesbury would refer to these drawings; the maid was then informed of the clothing and jewelry Eva planned to wear for the day.

Mrs. Stotesbury's Boudoir served as a workroom where she presided over the management of Whitemarsh Hall (as she did in her downstairs library, as well). The mansion had its own state-of-the-art phone exchange and operator, located in the basement, which were in constant use by Eva. Mr. Stotesbury's portrait, above the fireplace, was painted by Francois Flameng.

Primarily in Mrs. Stotesbury's Boudoir, but also in other parts of the mansion, there were numerous statuettes of birds. Eva had a fondness for these collectibles, along with a variety of fans. Examples can be seen here in the glass cases on either side of the doorway. A miniature boudoir on the third floor was designed by Eva for her granddaughter Louise Brooks.

The Boudoir led to a private retreat referred to as the Empire Loggia. Mrs. Stotesbury liked to explain to her friends that, because she often misplaced her eyeglasses, she had found it practical to order 52 pairs so she could keep one in each room that she used. She also kept a stockpile of $34 shaving brushes—one for each guest room—which were replaced when the guests left with them.

Part of Eva's Suite, this Breakfast Room provided a retreat for refreshment or afternoon tea. Eva's son, Jimmy, referring to his mother, commented, "She ran her household with more efficiency than any factory I was ever in." Regarding her role in entertaining, Eva would often say that "a nervous hostess makes an unhappy guest."

Returning down the hallway toward the east wing, one passed the guest suites facing the back of the estate. The Lacquer Guest Room was one of two rooms that featured beautiful, curved paneling with an inset for the bed. The second-floor rooms were constantly kept "on view," with doors open so visitors could see inside.

Maids were instructed to make sure that all personal effects be hidden from view. Because of the great number of drawers and furniture in each room, guests may have needed to search hard to find their belongings. The Apricot Room featured a recessed, wood-paneled wall with matching bookcases. When decorating the mansion, it was reported that Eva went to Philadelphia's largest bookstore and declared that she had "eight acres of shelves to fill, will you find me some nice books with beautiful bindings?"

The Blue Room also featured curved paneling. After three days of visiting, guests would receive an engraved card on their breakfast tray that asked if they were planning to leave by car or train. The card also noted that the secretary would be happy to book their reservations. This was Eva's not-so-subtle way of asking when the guests would be leaving.

This photograph was taken from the east end of the second-floor hallway. Looking out over the balcony, one could see down the staircase to the Entrance Hall, which was illuminated from the skylight above. Many guests complained that the formality of Whitemarsh Hall was not to their liking. Henry Ford once commented to reporters after a stay at the mansion, "The Stotesburys are charming people; it's a great experience to see how the rich live."

The William and Mary Room faced the front of the mansion and was located behind the service elevator and back staircase. Breakfast was always served to guests in their rooms; however, lunch and dinner were held in a variety of locations. This forced visitors to try numerous dining areas, and to listen for voices to determine where a meal was being served. Always punctual, E. T. was not very tolerant of guests arriving late to the table.

The Valley Suite was primarily used by Jimmy Cromwell. Eva's son was 25 when the mansion was finished; by that time he had married Delphine Dodge, heir to the Dodge auto fortune. He once commented, "I was born with a golden spoon in my mouth; the diamond cluster around it was added when my mother married Stotesbury." E. T. and Horace Dodge each contributed $50,000 per year to the couple as a wedding present.

Jimmy wed a total of four times, including his second marriage in 1935 to Doris Duke, heir to a tobacco fortune of $70 million. Jimmy's marital status could be determined at any time based on whether a double or two single beds were in the Valley Suite bedroom. During his bachelor periods, he usually resided in one of the houses located on the estate.

Mr. Stotesbury's Trophy Room was used to display the many ribbons and awards won by his trotters at various horse shows throughout the country. E. T. delighted in giving tours of the mansion, which always included the Trophy Room, the upstairs safe containing Eva's jewelry, and the wine cellar off the kitchen.

The Terrace Suite was used primarily by Eva's daughter Louise, who had married Walter Brooks, a well-to-do socialite from Baltimore, in 1908. They had two children who frequently stayed at Whitemarsh Hall. As a belated wedding present, E. T. had built the couple a $1 million mansion, Rainbow Hill, in Baltimore. However, Louise's jet-setting lifestyle and excessive spending had caused marital problems, and she and her husband were divorced in 1919.

This view reveals the Terrace Suite bathroom. In 1922, Louise married Gen. Douglas MacArthur, who also became a frequent guest at the mansion and was held in high esteem by Stotesbury. The marriage was doomed from the start, as Louise found it difficult to be the wife of a dedicated military officer. They were divorced in 1929. Louise ironically claimed a "failure to provide" in the divorce proceedings, in spite of her family's wealth.

The Terrace Suite was designed with a Loggia that was a match to Eva's Empire Loggia in the west wing. Louise was wed two more times, including a 10-year marriage to the English actor Lionel Atwell. MacArthur rarely spoke of his marriage to Louise, nor was it mentioned in the many biographical pieces that were written about him after he achieved international fame.

E. T. poses with the board members from the Philadelphia Union League. Stotesbury became a member in 1882 and served as president five times, before declining further office after 1923. During this time period, the members of the Union League "ran" Philadelphia politics. Stotesbury was a staunch Republican, contributing both his time and money to the political causes of the day. (Courtesy of Union League of Philadelphia.)

This photograph, taken c. July 1919, shows the partially completed Shady Garden prior to the mansion's opening in 1921. Also referred to as a *boulingrin* (a smooth-turf bowling green), this area was 200 feet long by 90 feet wide, and was located on the west side of the mansion. Greber created natural extensions to the mansion and combined elements of both English and French classical gardens to the design of the estate.

Here a 1936 party for leading Republican women is in full swing on the Back Terrace. The Lower Terrace gardens measured 200 feet by 100 feet, with fountains, gravel paths, and dwarf boxwoods taken from gardens once planted by Jerome Bonaparte, Napoleon's brother, in Woodbury, Maryland. Over the years, guests at the mansion included the king and queen of Sweden, Marshal Joseph Joffre (a World War I general), Pres. Warren Harding, Henry Ford, and Will Rogers.

This view from the Lower Terrace shows the *tapis vert* and beyond, extending over the Plaza and up to Willow Grove Avenue more than a mile away. When entering the estate, visitors were captured by the Georgian feel of a 300-acre English park. Only as they approached the mansion were they exposed to the formality and geometric lines of French classical landscaping.

This Belvedere was located at the southwest corner of the Lower Terrace. Greber's use of balustrades, fountains, statues, and stairways provided for a beautiful symmetry that highlighted and defined the natural gardens. On one occasion when the Stotesburys were entertaining, Eva had workers install colored lights in the fountains of the Upper and Lower Terrace gardens. A female guest remarked that the lighting reminded her of Coney Island. The colored lights were removed, and the guest was never invited back.

This rose garden was likely located near Graystone. The large house was situated on the estate, east of the back gardens of the mansion, and could be accessed from Cheltenham Avenue. It also had a detached stable and was used through the years by Jimmy Cromwell. Graystone burned in 1948, but the stables have survived.

This view from the *tapis vert* looks back toward the house and Upper Terraces. The floor of the *tapis vert* lay almost 20 feet below the Upper Terrace, and was accessible by pathways and a beautiful curved stairway that sheltered a recessed statue of Neptune. Landscape architect Greber's use of stairways and levels provided for constantly changing views and landscape designs.

Running parallel along the east side of the *tapis vert* was a 400-foot-long maple *allée*. A statue of Artemis stood at the head of Maple Alley, located at the southeastern corner of the mansion. When the mansion was built, most of the trees and shrubbery were planted fully grown.

This party took place on the Back Terrace in 1921. It was estimated that the Stotesburys entertained more than 100,000 guests at their three estates. Eva's hospitality was legendary, with tea for 600 or dinner for 40. John Russell, a famous New York furniture restorer, once commented on Whitemarsh Hall by saying, "I will tell you what it is, what style. It is pure twentieth-century American rich. And it is perfectly beautiful."

Four

THE BEGINNING
OF THE END

Prior to the stock-market crash and the resulting Depression, E. T. had begun to "live on fat." As his personal secretary at the time, Miss McBride, related, "He was invading his own principles," with his expenses exceeding his income. Stotesbury began to sell off his stocks and bonds and withdraw his equity in Drexel & Company. It is estimated that Stotesbury withdrew about $55 million between 1933 and 1938. He initially did this as an alternative to curtailing Eva's spending or cutting their generous contributions to charities. But after 1932, there would be a conscious controlling of expenses, and noticeable changes at Whitemarsh Hall. The Stotesburys now held only occasional dinners and parties, such as this one in 1934. From left to right are E. T., Miss Hester Laning, Mrs. Laning, Eva, and Vice Adm. Harris Laning. (Courtesy of Temple University Urban Archives.)

By 1932, the effects of the stock-market crash had taken a toll on Stotesbury's wealth. In spite of this, he did not call in most of his firm's loans. He had faith in people and their good name, believing that in time they would pay back the money that was owed. He also made new loans during this time to help floundering companies survive. What kept him from complete personal ruin was his diversification across investments. During this period, there was a growing resentment by the general public of the extraordinarily wealthy upper class, who were seemingly unaffected by the Depression. A Philadelphia radio commentator mentioned on his radio program the positive effects a bomb placed at Whitemarsh Hall would have. The Stotesburys then decided to close their three homes, dismiss the bulk of their staff, and take an "extended vacation" in Europe. This photograph and the next were both taken on December 18, 1932, while the Stotesburys were abroad. (Courtesy of Hagley Museum and Library.)

E. T. and his fellow bankers disliked FDR and his New Deal politics, which proposed the idea of redistributing wealth to help the masses. Stotesbury believed the Depression would cure itself in time, and that intelligence, ambition, and good character were all that were necessary for someone to achieve wealth. Unwilling to wait it out himself, Stotesbury turned over his paintings, tapestries, furniture, and porcelains to the Philadelphia Museum of Art for safekeeping, where this collection filled five galleries. On the morning the Stotesburys set sail, Eva said to their lawyer, "Well, Morris, if we never come back, we've had ten wonderful years of it." They left on the steamship *Rex* with Jimmy and a few of their trusted servants. The Stotesburys eventually missed the United States and returned home late in 1932, but they did not reopen Whitemarsh Hall until the fall of 1933. Continued fear of a class uprising saw four Thompson machine guns installed on the roof of Whitemarsh Hall. (Courtesy of Hagley Museum and Library.)

At the time this photograph was taken on May 1, 1936, the stock market had rallied somewhat, but was destined for a dramatic downturn in February 1937. In spite of E. T.'s attempts to counteract this crisis, he was no longer equipped to handle it because of the changing economic rules, his advanced age, and his diminishing mental acuity. Stotesbury was called before Congress to give an account of his business holdings, to determine if he and others like him had contributed to the stock-market crash and the Depression. Congressmen were surprised to learn that his wealth was not distributed among the giant corporations, but instead was diversified among more than 100 smaller companies. No blame was placed on Stotesbury as a result, but he resented the fact that he had even been under suspicion. (Courtesy of Hagley Museum and Library.)

This and the following five photographs were taken by gardener Marcel Duchamps c. 1935. By this time, the grounds immediately around Whitemarsh Hall and the road leading up to it, including the Plaza, were still well maintained, but the rest of the previously manicured estate was left to go to seed. E. T. rode around the property in his car to inspect the grounds, while Eva and Jimmy were known to walk for their review.

The servant staff was now maintained at a minimum, rooms were closed off in Whitemarsh Hall to save on heat and maintenance, and the fountains were turned on only for special occasions. Come springtime, Greber's exquisite parterres would not be replanted. In this image, staff members prepare the back gardens for the winter months. E. T. rented several homes on the property to his employees, including those on Plymouth Road, known today as Gladstone Road.

The trees and shrubbery around the mansion were individually covered to protect them from snow and ice. This photograph stands in stark contrast to the lush springtime scenes when everything is uncovered and in bloom. The full-time outside staff was reduced from about 70 to just 8 after the mansion reopened in 1933.

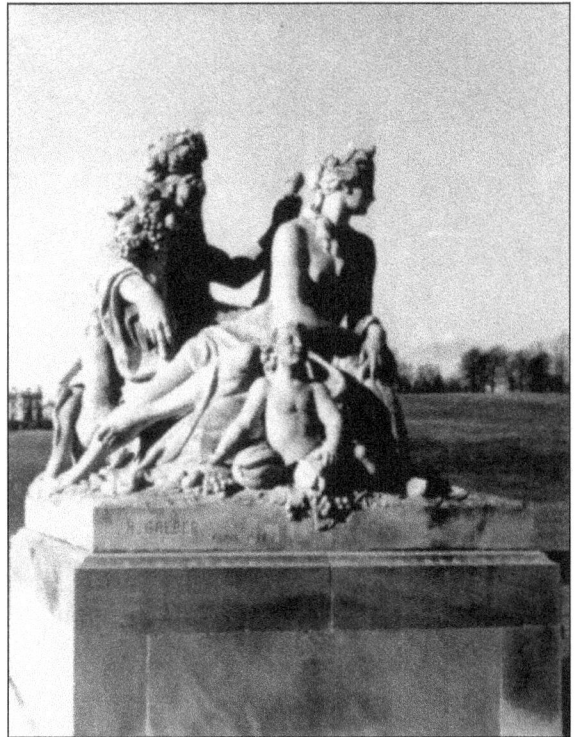

Adorning the Plaza there were complementary allegorical figures that were created in 1924 and 1925 by Jacques Greber's father, Henri-Léon. Connected by a balustrade retaining wall, the statues surrounded the central fountain. This statuary grouping could be seen from the mansion, but not from the main gates on Willow Grove Avenue, although it was situated directly between the two points.

These greenhouses were located on Cheltenham Avenue, near the David Steele house and between the later Widener and Patton Roads. Steele was hired originally to clear the land, and he was one of the last employees of the estate. Eva insisted that Steele's house and all surrounding buildings be painted green to blend in with the surroundings so they would not be obvious to the eye as one drove through the grounds to the mansion.

The main gatehouse at Willow Grove Avenue saw very little traffic in 1935. E. T.'s oldest daughter, Edith Lewis Stotesbury Hutchinson, died on May 20 at the age of 58. The Stotesburys took her death particularly hard and were in mourning for almost a year. There were no parties held at this time, and guests were limited to family and close friends. After the mourning period ended, the parties and dinners resumed, but much less frequently.

El Mirasol, meaning "The Sunflower" in Spanish, was the Stotesburys' winter home. Located at 348 North Ocean Boulevard, Palm Beach, Florida, it was designed by Addison Mizner. Construction lasted from 1918 until 1921, at a cost of about $1 million. The 37-room estate included a 40-car garage, an auditorium, and a private zoo. Eva died here in 1946; the property was sold the following year. Within a couple more years, a housing complex replaced the mansion.

Wingwood House, the Stotesburys' summer home, was on Eden Street in Bar Harbor, Maine. They purchased the original house in 1925, but promptly tore it down to build this larger home, which was designed by Magaziner, Eberhard, & Harris and cost more than $1 million. The 80-room mansion took two years to build and had a 500-foot frontage on Frenchman Bay. Standing in disrepair after Eva's death, Wingwood House was torn down in 1953 to make way for the Canadian National Bluenose ferry terminal.

Shown above is the first of two Stotesbury yachts, both named *Nedeva* after Edward's and Lucretia's combined nicknames. Eva would not step aboard the 70-foot *Nedeva* after a serious accident occurred as the Stotesburys were leaving port on one of their trips. Thereafter, she traveled by train, and E. T. used the yacht to travel between his properties. Each of their personal chauffeurs transported their private cars—hers a Rolls Royce, his a Buick—between the properties. E. T. also had a private Pullman car, called "the Frances," which he used for travel even prior to his marriage to Eva.

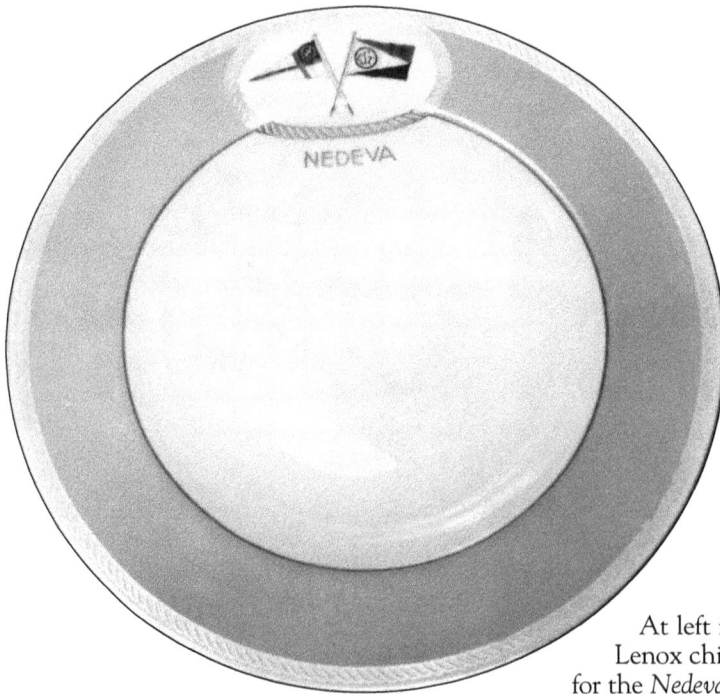

At left is a soup bowl from the set of Lenox china commissioned exclusively for the *Nedeva*. (Courtesy of Dan Helwig.)

Even during tough financial times, E. T. continued to donate his time and money to selected charities. One of his favorites was the Starr Garden Recreation Center in Philadelphia. In this photograph, taken during a December 27, 1926 Christmas party, he holds the attention of the young Boy Scout musicians. His grandson Walter Brooks Jr. recalled that it was embarrassing to arrive there in a chauffeur-driven car for this yearly event. Yet E. T. was very self-conscious about the great poverty around him and ordered all the whitewalls on his cars painted a less-impressive black. Even Eva cautioned her son, Jimmy: "Great wealth carries with it great responsibilities. It is the best part of the Christian ethic to take care of the underprivileged and less fortunate. Don't forget that if you don't, you may lose all your luxuries, because revolution is an indictment of the ruling class." (Courtesy of Historical Society of Pennsylvania.)

Likely taken outside St. Paul's Episcopal Church in Chestnut Hill, this photograph is typical of so many showing E. T. a step in front of Eva to offset his short stature. Knowing that E. T.'s money was what gained their acceptance in Philadelphia's high society, Eva admitted, "The only successful financial transaction I ever made in my life was when I married Mr. Stotesbury."

This image was taken on New Year's Eve 1937. Edward had only another five months to live. He was injured when he slipped and fell on the *Nedeva*, and was confined to bed with a special corps of nurses in constant attendance. All entertainment and business meetings were promptly cancelled. He experienced poor health all that season at *El Mirasol*, but rallied enough to travel to Whitemarsh Hall in mid-April via the *Nedeva*. (Courtesy of Temple University Urban Archives.)

E. T. was renowned for his love of playing the drums, whether at private parties or public functions. This image is one of few where he has let down his guard and is genuinely smiling and enjoying himself. He was a regular participant each year at Wyndmoor's Memorial Day parade, playing his drum as part of the activities.

On May 16, 1938, at 9:20 p.m., Edward T. Stotesbury died at Whitemarsh Hall. He had visited his offices at Drexel & Company and Reading Company earlier in the day, but suffered a heart attack while his chauffeur, John Kennedy, was driving him home. Doctors attended to Stotesbury, but after a nap and dinner, he collapsed and died in Eva's arms. He was to have played the drum at Memorial Day services in Wyndmoor. Pictured at the war memorial in Wyndmoor are C. W. Conyers (left) and John J. McCullough.

Arriving at the candle-lit funeral ceremony at Whitemarsh Hall were 300 people and 100 truckloads of flowers. E. T.'s casket was placed in the middle of the Ballroom on a bed of magnolias; a small drum draped in black was hung at the foot of the casket. Eva had issued a Western Union telegram asking her husband's friends to come to the ceremony "before he leaves his home forever." Here, Fairmount Park officers carry his casket at Woodlands Cemetery. (Courtesy of Temple University Urban Archives.)

The funeral procession left Whitemarsh Hall, traveled down Willow Grove Avenue, through Fairmount Park via Forbidden Drive, to Woodlands Cemetery. E. T. was buried in the Thomas P. Stotesbury family plot with his first wife, daughter Helen, parents, and siblings. Rev. Malcolm E. Peabody, rector of St. Paul's Episcopal Church of Chestnut Hill, conducted the service. E. T.'s headstone is a testament to a man born and raised in the modest Quaker tradition, in spite of his later lavish lifestyle. (Courtesy of Deborah C. Wilson.)

Five

AFTER THE STOTESBURYS

E. T.'s will specified that the English portraits, tapestries, the two sets of furniture, the great Isfahan rug in the Ballroom, and the porcelains from Duveen be sold. Everything else was left to Eva, along with lifetime use of their three mansions. Stotesbury's estate at his death was estimated at about $4 million, but a year later a more detailed accounting set it at about $10 million. Without enough money to keep the three homes open and maintained, Eva promptly closed Whitemarsh Hall and put it up for sale. She was also forced to dismiss her staff of 40, many of whom had followed her seasonally from house to house. This photograph was taken in the spring of 1939, just several months after E. T.'s death. With the Stotesburys no longer returning, the house is closed, the shades drawn, and the landscaping left ragged. Whitemarsh Hall already has a vacant and lonely feel to it. (Courtesy of Temple University Urban Archives.)

Stogdell Stokes and Fiske Kimball of the Philadelphia Museum of Art visited Whitemarsh Hall to meet with Eva before she moved to Washington. She said, "I thought I must sell the sculpture, but at the figures I am offered, I would much rather give it to the Museum in memory of Ned." And so, Eva donated the four stone statues by Pajou, the marble by Tassaert, and the two Clodion groups. Pictured is the original sales brochure for the real estate. (Courtesy of ATOFINA Chemicals.)

WHITEMARSH·HALL

"The Versailles of America"

Estate of the late Edward T. Stotesbury
near Chestnut Hill, Philadelphia, Pa.
overlooking Whitemarsh Valley

Eva left Whitemarsh Hall forever, publicly stating, "I would be too unhappy living in Philadelphia without Mr. Stotesbury." Truthfully, she never was at home in Philadelphia, having privately commented in the past, "I stay here only because of Ned. Philadelphia is Ned's town. I really don't like it much." Eva moved in to Marly in Washington, D.C. (it too a Trumbauer design), and rented the house from Anna Dodge Dillman for a nominal sum.

In support of the war effort, in 1942 Eva donated the two miles of eight-foot-high wrought-iron fencing that surrounded much of Whitemarsh Hall, to be melted down for the creation of armaments. Eva's contribution came to 395 tons of scrap that could be used to make 18,000 guns. Looking northward, this view reveals a section of fencing along Cheltenham Avenue, with the mansion on top of the hill.

During World War II, a great fear erupted that the Germans would bomb major East Coast cities. As a result, many of America's public treasures were moved to private residences further inland. New York's Metropolitan Museum of Art elected to store its own works in Whitemarsh Hall, under armed guards. The collection remained here until the spring of 1944.

Whitemarsh Hall stood unoccupied for five years after Eva's departure. Judging from the neglect of the gardens, this photograph was likely taken during that period. Eva did return to Philadelphia in 1939 to view her donated sculptures in the Philadelphia Museum of Art; however, she left the city without visiting Whitemarsh Hall. The mansion was advertised in *Fortune* magazine, but no sale resulted. (Courtesy of Free Library of Philadelphia.)

Eva Stotesbury, seen here with Jimmy, died of a coronary thrombosis at *El Mirasol* on May 23, 1946. She was 81. After her first heart attack, Eva said, "My dear son, I am yearning for my quiet grave. I don't want any part of your world, Mr. Roosevelt's world, or Mr. Stalin's world." Funeral services were held at *El Mirasol*, and Eva was buried in Chicago's Oak Woods Cemetery, in the Roberts family plot. (Courtesy of Richard C. Marchand.)

The Pennsylvania Salt Manufacturing Company purchased Whitemarsh Hall and the surrounding 38 acres in October 1943 for $167,000. This was less than the sum the New York Metropolitan Museum of Art had spent to outfit the mansion to store its artwork during the war years. The company converted the formal Entrance Hall (above), which once welcomed American and European royalty, into a more conservative entranceway for greeting customers and other visitors (below). Note the information display of the company's products and the closet to the left of the fireplace, which was converted into a receptionist's room with a telephone switchboard. In 1957, the company changed its name to Pennsalt Chemicals Corporation, commonly shortened to Pennsalt. Today, after several mergers and acquisitions, it is known as ATOFINA Chemicals. (Below, courtesy of ATOFINA Chemicals.)

The Stotesburys' Reception Room (left), just off of the Main Entrance Hall, where so many notable guests through the years had waited to greet their hosts and check their coats and hats, was transformed into a conference room (below). Gone are the Oriental rug, the magnificent tapestries adorning the walls, and the chandelier. Replacing the exquisite, formal furniture are the relatively Spartan accommodations where Pennsalt's executives met. (Below, courtesy of ATOFINA Chemicals.)

The Gallery Hall connected the Ballroom to the East and West Rotundas. Originally housing statuary such as the Clodion piece seen here in the mansion's heyday (right), the area was used by Pennsalt for secretarial and clerical offices (below). At the far west end of this series of hallways, the Tea Room was converted into a laboratory to handle radioactive materials. Although the Stotesburys did not live at Whitemarsh Hall during the summer months, they had installed a rudimentary, but effective, form of air-conditioning to protect their artwork from heat and humidity. The Pennsalt employees truly benefitted, as they worked here year round. (Below, courtesy of ATOFINA Chemicals.)

The Stotesburys' Living Room (above), also known as the Drawing Room, was converted into an extensive laboratory. As seen in the photograph below, the fireplace opening has been closed up, and the exquisite mantle and framing for the portrait have been disassembled, crated, and moved to an off-site Pennsalt warehouse. Chandeliers have been replaced by suspended fluorescent lighting, and the bookshelves are now filled with chemical materials and artifacts. Just outside of this room, Pennsalt tunneled under the outside Terrace, all the way to the open Belvedere, to create additional laboratories for testing insecticides. Insects were ordered by the thousands and were delivered live through the mail. On one occasion, a shipment sent to an area post office was accidentally opened, and company officials were dispatched to dispose of the swarming creatures. (Below, courtesy of ATOFINA Chemicals.)

A typical lab such as this one was outfitted for compressed air, vacuums, natural gas, distilled and non-distilled water, low-pressure steam, 120- and 240-volt electricity, and some special gases. E. T. had required the installation of firefighting apparatus at Whitemarsh Hall, so the house had previously been equipped with two-inch water pipes throughout and fire extinguishers hidden but accessible behind wall panels. (Courtesy of ATOFINA Chemicals.)

The Stotesburys' Ballroom, designed for dancing and entertaining, was converted into Pennsalt's library for the chemists to conduct their reading and research. This view is of the east end of the former Ballroom, where there were seating areas for reading, with the head librarian stationed at the west end. Gone are the chandeliers, paintings, tapestries, porcelains, and the Oriental carpet, all replaced with institutional furnishings. (Courtesy of ATOFINA Chemicals.)

Eva's Suite of rooms, including the Loggia pictured above—once resplendent with its inlaid floor, chandelier, draperies, priceless statuary, and furniture—were stripped and transformed into organic chemistry laboratories (below). Eva's Bathroom became the first-aid station, with beds built across both the bathtub and the sink. E. T.'s Bathroom was outfitted with a spectrograph, and his Dressing Room was turned into an optics room. His closets, which once held more than 100 pair of shoes, were now lined with optical materials and supplies. (Below, courtesy of ATOFINA Chemicals.)

The Apricot Guest Room (above), which once provided guests with a beautiful view of the Back Terrace and gardens, was transformed into a laboratory (below), as were the other guest rooms. The recessed bookshelves and the wooden panel behind the bed's headboard have been removed to provide chemical storage space. A wooden panel to the right of the bed appears to have been removed as well, to provide access to the storage area behind this room. Pennsalt was meticulous when removing any piece of the house for alterations, such as crown moldings to run the pipes from room to room. Each item was catalogued and packed into a crate for off-site storage. In this way, theoretically, the house could have been restored to its original state upon Pennsalt's departure. (Below, courtesy of ATOFINA Chemicals.)

The Pennsalt sign posted on the wall in the photograph above humorously lists this as the "Whitemarsh Canteen," with food prices written in below. The serving area was located in the Stotesburys' first-floor Pantry area. Pennsalt employees ate in the adjoining east-side Summer Loggia (pictured below). In the mid-1950s, the kitchen and eating areas were moved to the third floor, after extensive renovations had removed most of the interior walls on that floor to create much-needed space. The third floor had originally contained bedrooms and bathrooms for the servants and the grandchildren, a sewing room, a cedar closet, a trunk room, secretaries' offices, linen closets, and additional storage space. (Courtesy of ATOFINA Chemicals.)

The west-side Arcade Loggia, also called the Orangerie (right), was converted into a power plant and pressure-reaction area (below). After chemical compounds were tested in small amounts in the laboratories, further tests on 100 pounds of the material would be conducted in this area. The end walls of the Belvedere were enclosed with two-foot-thick barriers, which were filled with sand to dampen any explosions that might occur. The area was later rebuilt in the back gardens, away from the house. The first night-watchman's apartment was located in this wing until c. 1954, when it was moved to the third floor. (Below, courtesy of ATOFINA Chemicals.)

Formal gardens, pools and terraces surround the mansion-turned-workshop near Chestnut Hill, a suburb of Philadelphia.

Pennsalt employees enjoy a walk through the back gardens. As part of the purchase agreement, Pennsalt retained Henry DeLocke, the Stotesburys' assistant gardener, who, with a half-dozen helpers, maintained terraces, shrubs, and flower beds. It took two men a week just to keep the grass around the mansion cut. This photograph was likely taken prior to 1951, as the Orangerie doors are screened off but not yet enclosed for the power plant. (Courtesy of ATOFINA Chemicals.)

Pennsalt installed gas pumps at the head of Maple Alley, by the statue of Artemis. Stotesbury's original gas pumps for his fleet of automobiles were located away from the house, on land Pennsalt did not own. Notice the station wagon that the company used to bus its employees to and from the Chestnut Hill West railroad station. Refer to page 72 for a similar, earlier view. (Courtesy of ATOFINA Chemicals.)

This photograph was taken during the later years of Pennsalt's occupancy. The company did continue to rent the greenhouses on the left after selling the property. The structure built on the Upper Terrace, near the back of the house, was constructed in 1960, when Pennsalt entered the plastics field, for product research on Kynar® polyvinylidene fluoride resin. The power plant has been moved to the back garden area, along the retaining wall on the right.

Pennsalt receives visitors at Whitemarsh Hall in 1954. Seniors from the North East Catholic High School in Philadelphia, studying for careers in chemistry and medicine, toured the laboratories. Administrative assistant Norman Peschko addresses the group in the lobby. Around this time, Pennsalt underwent considerable expansion and reconfigured the mansion's facilities. (Courtesy of ATOFINA Chemicals.)

In 1946, most of the Stotesburys' original 300-acre tract was sold to Matthew H. McCloskey Jr. for a development of single-family homes to be known as Whitemarsh Village. This 1,000-home development was intended for returning servicemen and was priced accordingly at $8,800 to $9,800 per home. The road names of Whitemarsh Village memorialized figures famous during Whitemarsh Hall's heyday. The homes in the immediate foreground front on Stotesbury Avenue, and the first visible residential road in front of the mansion is Cromwell Road. The streets to the left of the mansion are Tyson and Delphine Roads. Patton and Widener Roads are seen behind the mansion. McCloskey was previously known as the developer of Philadelphia's Schuylkill Expressway. By 1963, Pennsalt had moved the last of its divisions to its new King of Prussia location, vacating Whitemarsh Hall for good. Although the mansion remained empty for a year before a buyer was found, Pennsalt continued to heat it in the winter months.

Pictured is the sales brochure issued in 1963. In July 1964, the mansion and 38 surrounding acres were sold to Willow Associates of Norristown for $350,000. Co-partnered by Sidney Dvorak, who stated that the property was purchased as "a long-term investment," the firm's intention was to find an owner who would utilize and preserve the grand structure and keep it intact for permanent use, such as a convent, college, nursing home, conference center, or township administrative headquarters. (Courtesy of ATOFINA Chemicals.)

FOR SALE
SUBURBAN PHILADELPHIA
(MINUTES FROM THE PENNSYLVANIA TURNPIKE)

LAND: 38 ACRES, HIGH, BEAUTIFULLY PLANTED, MAGNIFICENT GARDENS AND FOUNTAINS.

BUILDING: 50,000 SQ. FT. SUITABLE FOR OFFICES, RESEARCH, SCHOOLS AND OTHER INSTITUTIONAL USES. 34,000 SQ. FT. BASEMENT AND SAFE KEEPING SPACE. 9,000 SQ. FT. AUXILIARY BUILDINGS.

CONSTRUCTION: FIREPROOF CONSTRUCTION, 2 PASSENGER AND 1 FREIGHT ELEVATORS.

PRICE: OFFERED AT A FRACTION OF ITS ORIGINAL MULTI-MILLION DOLLAR COST IN 1920.

INDUSTRIAL-COMMERCIAL

Surpass Realty Co.
REALTORS

BROKERS
APPRAISERS
BUILDERS
INVESTORS

Prepared & Printed By
RMSI

While Willow Associates continued to explore viable long-term uses of Whitemarsh Hall, the firm hosted several interim activities, such as summer day camps and student art shows. The particular event depicted here was a public art show to benefit the National Multiple Sclerosis Society in October 1965. Two different night-watchmen were employed to protect the property through these years, the first of which was Jake Stanmier, followed by George Stone.

Willow Associates spent considerable money to maintain the mansion, as documented by invoices paid for elevator certification, electricity and water, grass cutting, pumping water out of the basement, repair of the copper roof, and rainspout cleaning. In 1969, the mansion's fire escapes were removed and the windows and doors were boarded up to prevent continued vandalism. After five years of searching for a buyer who would preserve the mansion and property, Willow Associates put it up for auction. (Courtesy of Donna Dvorak.)

On October 8, 1969, about 150 people gathered for the auction of Whitemarsh Hall. Auctioneer Alfred Traiman joked, "I'm sure you know that all it needs is a little sweeping and dusting." The slow-paced auction culminated in a winning bid by Kenneth Kaiserman and George Neff. Kaiserman stated that the house would not be demolished if they could help it, and the sale was finalized on December 8, 1969, for $552,000.

Six

THE END OF AN ERA

By June 1977, the once-palatial estate of Edward Stotesbury had been reduced to 46 acres surrounding a vandalized and dilapidated structure that was beyond any hope of restoration. When Kaiserman and Neff purchased the estate, they indicated that they would try to rehabilitate the mansion. But by 1972, plans had still not been formalized for what to do with the property. The township commissioners could not agree on the types of dwellings proposed by the developers—high-rise units, single homes, or townhouses. Local residents were frustrated that nothing was being done to remove the mansion, which by then had been consumed by fire, vandalism, and decay.

As the years wore on, the mansion fell into further ruin. The copper roof had been stolen, resulting in internal water damage. Statuary, fountains, and windows had been broken. Walnut doors, marble fireplaces, and gold faucets had been stripped. Although some township residents held out hope, the majority of people realized that the time had passed for any prospect of restoring the mansion, and that the only logical option was demolition. In 1976, developers proposed a plan to build 249 townhouses, after the township commissioners had previously rejected a plan for a 570-unit, high-rise condominium development. Many residents, with support from the Pennsylvania Historic and Museum Commissioners Office for Historic Preservation, still fought to preserve and restore the mansion, but no viable plans were presented for raising the funds to do so.

Whitemarsh Hall was not the only estate in the township to succumb to neglect and ruin. This photograph, taken in 1962 from a smashed window in the old Lea mansion, looked out over the valley to Whitemarsh Hall, which at the time was the headquarters of the Pennsylvania Salt Company. The Lea mansion was demolished in the mid-1960s, along with other fine homes such as the Newbold estate. These properties could not be saved from the ravages of time and from the lack of vision to provide for their preservation. (Courtesy of Drew Wagner.)

This image depicts one of the many calls local fire departments made to extinguish blazes started by arsonists and vandals at Whitemarsh Hall in the mid- to late-1970s. The marble around the fireplaces in the Ballroom had not yet been looted, but the damage and decay were all too obvious.

What was once the Entrance Hall (see page 48) was as gutted and ruined as the rest of the building. In the early months of 1978, the mansion and property had been purchased by Jay Gross. A local developer who had grown up in Whitemarsh Village, Gross planned to build 183 townhouse units. The mansion would be demolished, and the three levels below ground would be filled in to create open space for neighborhood use.

In this photograph of the west side of the Entrance Hall, one can still see the remains of the fireplace, above which had once hung the portrait of Edward Stotesbury. The entranceway into the Ballroom now hid the recessed pocket door, which had been moved back into the wall and sealed during the Pennsalt years. This door, never discovered by vandals or looters, was later recovered during demolition.

This view of the west side of the Ballroom looks down the Organ Hall (through the doorway on the right), where the pipe organ had once played "The End of a Perfect Day." When the copper roof was torn off by looters in the early 1970s, the resulting water damage further sealed the fate of the mansion, melting plaster ceilings and ornate moldings. Because entry into the mansion was easily accessible through the Back Terrace in the Ballroom, these first-floor rooms suffered heavy damage from vandalism and graffiti.

Taken from the Drawing Room, this photograph looks eastward through E. T.'s library into the Ballroom. The damage and senseless destruction were difficult to comprehend in a place once known for such beauty and refinement. Memories of grand balls and opulent parties were now only haunting reminders of a time long past.

By the 1970s, Mr. Stotesbury's Library was just a shell of brick and molding plaster. Prior to demolition, anything of value was removed, including the beautiful wood paneling and the marble fireplace that once adorned this room (see page 51). This view shows the entranceway that leads into the Grand Ballroom.

This view of the Billiard Room looks into the entranceway to the East Rotunda. Gone are the paintings by Romney, Gainsborough, and Reynolds—a collection of English art considered one of the finest in the world. Also vanished are the walnut paneling and polished hardwood floor. Time had reduced this room to a shell of rotted wood and peeling plaster.

In early 1980, Geppert Brothers of Colmar was awarded the contract to raze the mansion and fill in the underground basements to ground level. Geppert estimated that demolition would take about a month, because usable materials would be salvaged for resale. Demolition began April 1, 1980, and lasted through mid-May. The mansion had been well built; although it finally succumbed to the pounding of the wrecking ball, it proved difficult to bring down even after years of abuse.

In this photograph of the east side of the mansion during demolition, the service entrance is filled in with rubble; the side Terrace and Loggia having already been demolished. The contractors razed the mansion starting with the outside wings, then worked from the back to the front, salvaging the iron beams for scrap and filling in the underground levels as they proceeded.

The limestone statue of Artemis stands in ruin amid the overgrown shrubbery and woods along the east side and near the service entrance. Gas pumps, once located here to provide fuel for Pennsalt's fleet of automobiles, had long ago been removed. Gone are the trimmed boxwood hedges, gravel walkways, and Norwegian maples seen on page 72.

This photograph captures a view of the back of the house prior to demolition. The boarded-up windows have been opened, allowing light into the mansion for the last time. The balustrade on the third floor has been mostly removed, showing the windows of what had been the servants' quarters. Here, the Stotesbury grandchildren had once played on the third-floor Terrace, while royalty and the elite were entertained on the patio below.

112

Shown here are the remains of the Terrace Suite Loggia prior to demolition. With its ornate plaster ceiling and tiled floor long ruined, the suite of rooms where Gen. and Mrs. Douglas MacArthur once stayed (see page 68) are but a memory soon to be reduced to dust.

This image of the back of the mansion provides an additional view of the second-floor Terrace Suite Loggia. Below this was the Dining Room, from whence one looked over the Back Terrace and formal gardens. The Orangerie, extending out from the east wing, was originally designed as an open veranda and breezeway, but had been enclosed during the Pennsalt years to provide for storage.

On the west side, the first-floor Loggia and Terraces were also removed prior to razing the main part of the house. The Belvedere in the background, saved from the wrecking ball, is one of the few remaining structures on the grounds today.

This cutaway view of the mansion shows the front and eastern sides of the house after demolition of the east wing. The archway from the East Rotunda into the hallway is revealed on the first floor. To the right of this would have been the Billiard Room, with the remains of the entrance and fireplace still visible in the brick wall. The entire second-floor wing, which included Jimmy Cromwell's Valley Suite and the Terrace Suite, are gone; only the arched doorway to the second-floor hallway remains at this point.

The first-floor remains of the East Rotunda appear in the foreground in this view of the mansion's eastern side. Revealed on the third floor are the remains of the Main Hall and servants' quarters that looked out toward the rear of the property. The massive steel-and-brick infrastructure of the mansion, once hidden by ornate plaster moldings, marble, and wood paneling, tried stubbornly to withstand the pounding of the wrecking ball in a final act of defiance.

Jay Gross had planned to retain the mansion's portico and 50-foot-high limestone columns, along with some other architectural remains, in order to give the community a sense of the history and grandeur that was once Whitemarsh Hall. Although the portico was not able to be preserved, the columns still stand to this day as a reminder of what once occupied this hill.

Demolition continued inward to the main part of the mansion, as this view of the east side shows a large opening in the second-floor stairway and Entrance Hall. The remains of the second-floor ceiling show the skylight that had been installed at a significant cost after the house was constructed, per Eva's orders, to allow more natural light into the entryway on the first floor.

This photograph allows a closer look at the skylight on the second-floor ceiling, with a view through to the attic and roof. At the time it was constructed, Whitemarsh Hall was considered the most expensive residence ever built in the state. In 1970, an estimate revealed that it would have cost $12 million to build again.

The last rooms standing on the first floor were the Entrance Hall and Ballroom, shown here in this eastward view through the arches that once led to the Rotunda and Breakfast Room. During demolition of the mansion, a hidden wall safe was uncovered in the Breakfast Room. There was a lot of excitement about what might be found in it—money, jewelry? But once opened, the safe was revealed to contain only paperwork on Stotesbury's thoroughbred horses.

This photograph shows the center section of the mansion, with the Grotto in the foreground. The fountains and pools had long before stopped running, leaving stagnant ponds overgrown with weeds and rubbish. A tunnel led from one of the basements all the way out to a backyard along Patton Road, where a locked gate barred the entrance. Legend states that this was built as an exit for partygoers during Prohibition days.

The pocket door that led from the Entrance Hall to the Ballroom is excavated from the remains of the mansion. This door had been recessed into the wall (see page 48) and sealed by Pennsalt, and was discovered just prior to the demolition of the Ballroom and remaining structure. The door was recovered in perfect condition, glass intact and paint untouched by time. (Courtesy of John Deming.)

What had taken four years and $3 million to build was brought down in six weeks. A journalist once said that Whitemarsh Hall "will remain many decades a point to which visitors will motor in order to fill their minds with a conception of the luxuriance and distinction that can be created by immense wealth." Ironically, the house served the wealthy for only 17 years, with the last decade of its life being spent in absolute ruin.

Seven

EPILOGUE

Two years after Jay Gross purchased Whitemarsh Hall, and just prior to his demolition of the mansion, this sign on Cheltenham Avenue advertised the upcoming townhouse development. It was very simply and tastefully named Stotesbury. Original plans to rebuild Greber's gardens, and to add a swimming pool and tennis courts, would not be realized, although Gross did retain some elements of the earlier splendor. He built only a third of the homes before construction stopped for two years. Subsequently, Evans Builders purchased the property and constructed the remaining two-thirds of the development. The street names also paid tribute to Whitemarsh Hall's heyday: Trumbauer and Duveen Drives, and Trumbauer and Clodion Courts.

The entire Stotesbury Townhouse complex is revealed in this aerial view. The main entrance to the development, Trumbauer Drive, comes in from the upper right corner, as it enters the complex from Cheltenham Avenue. Also seen here are Whitemarsh Hall's entranceway columns on the left side, the garden retaining wall in the middle, and a partially visible Belvedere below the retaining wall. Refer to page 42 for an earlier, slightly similar view. (Courtesy of CSK Management.)

Two lonely sentinels still mark what was the main entrance to Whitemarsh Hall on Willow Grove Avenue, although the wrought-iron gates have long since been removed. The crushed white gravel of the mansion's heyday has been replaced by the paved Douglas Road, which was named after Gen. Douglas MacArthur and is the main entry road into Whitemarsh Village. More than six decades of residential growth since E. T.'s death have obscured most of the hilltop view where the mansion was once visible a mile away.

The 85-year-old gatehouse on Willow Grove Avenue has been lovingly restored in recent years. Additions include a lawn, a pair of handsome entrance pillars, and a wrought-iron fence, representative of the original eight-foot-high fence that had surrounded the entire estate. Refer to page 80 for an earlier view. (Courtesy of Deborah C. Wilson.)

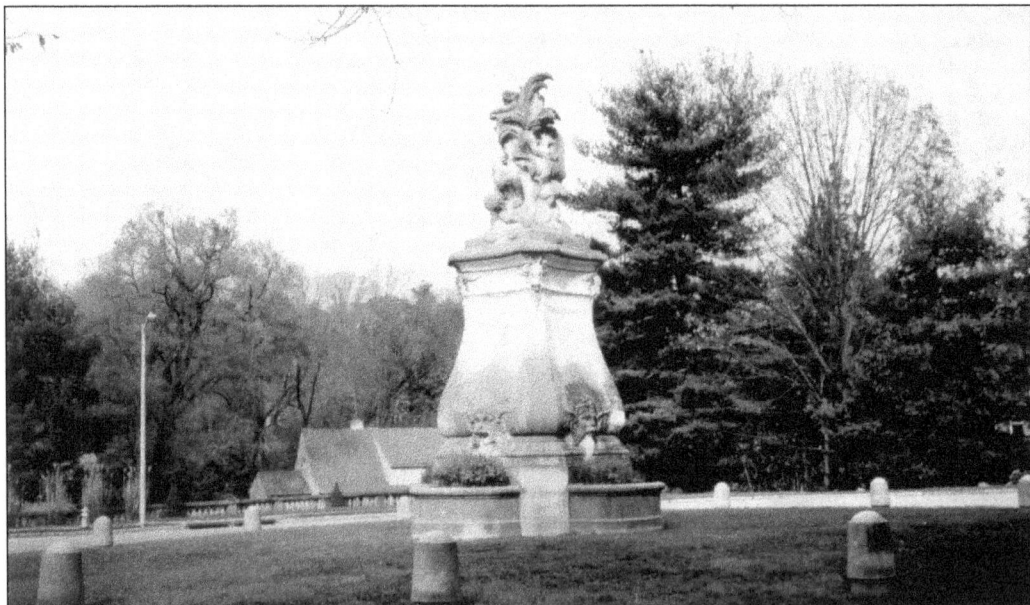

The Plaza is now known as Claridge Circle, bisecting Widener and Claridge Roads. Fortunately, the main statuary has not only survived, but is now the centerpiece for neighborhood block parties. Area residents regularly plant flowers in the four fountain bowls, and the township maintains the surrounding grass. The remaining Henri-Léon Greber statuary, just out of view to the left of this image, is cared for and decorated seasonally by a young woman who lives next to it. (Courtesy of Deborah C. Wilson.)

Located along Cheltenham Avenue is the only remaining wrought-iron fencing on what was the original Whitemarsh Hall property. Shown here is a former service entrance to the mansion; the road ran under Maple Alley and terminated at the east-side servants' wing seen on page 25. Original homes remaining on the property include the Bungalow on Paper Mill Road, which housed Stotesbury's chauffeurs, and former Mitchell Harrison homes.

Another service entrance into Whitemarsh Hall, located off Paper Mill Road, is today a private residence. Built between 1893 and 1897, it was originally the main entrance to the Robert Grant Fell estate, later purchased by E. T. and used as housing for his on-site servants and groundskeepers. The entrance door to the tower is several feet off the ground, so that the gatekeeper could open the doors of incoming carriages and greet and identify the guests.

The original two miles of wrought-iron fencing around the Whitemarsh Hall property had several smaller entrance and exit openings. This gateway was given to the township when Eva donated the fencing to the government for the war effort. It currently serves as the entranceway to the Springfield Township Police firing range on Wissahickon Avenue.

Developer Jay Gross grew up on Gladstone Road, formerly named Plymouth Road, on the Stotesbury estate. Later, he took advantage of Springfield Township's new cluster-zoning provision to begin building the 183-unit Stotesbury Townhouse complex. Township commissioners required that the mansion be demolished and the belowground floors be filled in. This view looks at Whitemarsh Hall's former entranceway, with the mansion now removed. (Courtesy of Deborah C. Wilson.)

The West Terrace walkway, which originally led from the Tea Room and the Drawing Room to the open Belvedere, remains today, minus the balustrade on the left side that overlooked the Upper Terrace gardens. The chandelier that once adorned the inside of this Belvedere is also long gone, but one can still imagine the grandeur of the past when standing in this structure and gazing out over the former gardens. (Courtesy of Deborah C. Wilson.)

This group of townhouses stands in what was once a heavily wooded area bordering the white-gravel walkways of the formal gardens. Although the figures are not adjusted for inflation, it is interesting to note that today one of these middle-class townhouses sells for more than what Pennsalt paid for the unblemished mansion and its surrounding acreage in 1943. (Courtesy of Deborah C. Wilson.)

Trees in the former Maple Alley were removed to allow construction of these townhouses. The homes' backyards abut the garden retaining wall, where the upper balustrades have been removed. The ground level of the former garden area has been raised several feet, burying the lower stairs that originally reached the top of the wall. Refer to page 30 for an earlier view. (Courtesy of Deborah C. Wilson.)

The former site of the formal gardens and mansion is designated today as a common area for the Stotesbury townhouse owners to enjoy. The ground level has been raised so that the pools that once stood in front of the Grotto are now covered. This photograph is in stark contrast to similar ones taken during the mansion's heyday, as seen on page 71. (Courtesy of Deborah C. Wilson.)

When the Stotesburys were deciding on the site for their home, one can only guess that they chose this location because they could look out for miles over the farmlands of the Whitemarsh Valley from their front door. The view today, looking in the same direction, is obscured by the residential development and growth of trees that replaced the fields of the farming communities of 80 years ago. (Courtesy of Deborah C. Wilson.)

Through the years, township residents and non-residents alike have visited the house and grounds of Whitemarsh Hall. These have included children sledding the hills in winter, families picnicking on the lawn in summer, and the curiosity seekers arriving daily. In this photograph, the authors' family, who resided in Whitemarsh Village, visit the mansion *c*. 1958. Edward C. Zwicker III is seen with his sister Deborah Carol (Zwicker) Wilson in the Grotto. (Courtesy of E. C. Zwicker III.)

During their year of research, the authors were entertained with numerous Whitemarsh Hall stories and memories from many people. This book has been made possible because of all the people who so willingly shared their own research, stories, photographs, and documents. Authors Ed and Charles Zwicker, pictured in the Grotto today, hope that this book will form the basis for additional volumes on Whitemarsh Hall in the future for many generations to come. (Courtesy of Deborah C. Wilson.)

ACKNOWLEDGMENTS

The authors and the Springfield Township Historical Society are proud to work with Arcadia Publishing, for the second time in two years, on this pictorial history of Whitemarsh Hall. It was made possible largely by people who have a profound passion for Edward Stotesbury and his "Versailles of America," and who were willing to share their own collections of photographs and information and, just as importantly, their time, to help produce the first published book dedicated solely to Whitemarsh Hall. We are greatly indebted to the following individuals: John Deming, Donna Dvorak, Robert Hibbert, Richard C. Marchand, Joseph Timoney, and Cintra and Wayne Willcox.

The following institutions also contributed images and information to this volume: ATOFINA Chemicals, formerly Pennsalt (Susan Hunsicker); the Chestnut Hill Historical Society (Rosemary Lord); the Free Library of Philadelphia (Janine Pollock and David DuPuy); the Hagley Museum (Barbara Hall); the Historical Society of Pennsylvania (Kerry McLaughlin and Dr. Daniel N. Rolph); the Library Company of Philadelphia (Sarah Weatherwax); the Pennsylvania State Archives (Mike Sherbon); the Philopatrian Literary Institute (Clyde Hancox); the Stotesbury Townhouse Association (Zeke Kaplan of CSK Management); the Temple University Urban Archives (Evan Towle); and the Union League of Philadelphia (James G. Mundy Jr.).

Several individuals who are no longer with us contributed greatly to the collection of materials on the Stotesburys and Whitemarsh Hall, which served as invaluable references. They include Alfred S. Branam Jr., Tom Dillon, Sidney T. Dvorak, and Marie Kitto.

Additional references offering valuable information included the following: *American Splendor: The Residential Architecture of Horace Trumbauer* by Michael C. Kathrens; *Twilight of Splendor* by James T. Maher; the unpublished work *The Little King—The Life and Times of Edward T. Stotesbury* by John Aaron; and the Whitemarsh Hall Internet site of Gerry Serianni (www.serianni.com/wh.htm).

Special thanks go to Edna Jones, who tirelessly edited our work; to Deborah Wilson, who helped with research and photography; to Dan Helwig for photographs of Stotesbury memorabilia; to Craig Seltzer for photographs of Edward Stotesbury and Horace Trumbauer; to Edward C. Zwicker III for artwork; and to those people who live today on the original Stotesbury estate and work tirelessly to preserve what remains of it: the gatehouses, the Plaza statuary, the pre-Stotesbury-era homes, and the remains of the great house itself.

The authors would like to dedicate this book to the next generation of their family, who will be the ones to help carry on the history: Charles's children, Charles Guenst Jr. and Meghan Rose, and Ed's daughter Jessie Leah and granddaughter McKayla Jade.

www.ingramcontent.com/pod-product-compliance
Lightning Source LLC
Chambersburg PA
CBHW050705150426
42813CB00055B/2530